THE ETERNAL QUEST

Extemporaneous talks given by Osho
in Mumbai, India

OSHO

The Eternal Quest

by Osho

Editing: Satyam
Design: Khushi
Typesetting: Sonar
Production: Kamaal

A REBEL BOOK
REBEL is an imprint of OSHO Multimedia & Resorts Pvt. Ltd.,
17 Koregaon Park, Pune 411001 MS, India

Copyright © 1967, 2008 OSHO International Foundation
www.osho.com/copyrights

All rights reserved. No part of this book may be reproduced or transmitted in any form or by any means, electronic or mechanical, including photocopying, recording, or by any information storage and retrieval system, without prior written permission from OSHO International Foundation.

OSHO is a registered trademark of OSHO International Foundation, used under license. www.osho.com/trademarks

Photos: Courtesy OSHO International Foundation

The material in this book is transcribed from a selection of individual talks by Osho given to live audiences. These talks are compiled and published under the title, *The Eternal Quest*. Some of this new selection is also available as original audio recordings. Text and audio recordings can be found via the online OSHO Library at www.osho.com/library

Printed in India by Thomson Press (India) Ltd., New Delhi

ISBN 81-7261-221-4
ISBN 978-81-7261-221-4

In loving gratitude to Osho from Darshan

CONTENTS

	Preface	viii
1	Religion: Knowing through Feeling	1
2	Discovering Your Own Path	9
3	The Twenty-first Century Approach to Meditation	37
4	Hatha Yoga and Hypnosis	53
5	First Freedom, Then Expression	67
6	Consciousness: Living in the Vertical Dimension	89
7	The Disease Called Seriousness	111
8	God: The Creative Process, Not the Creator	119
9	The Need for Authenticity	137

10	Life: Uncharted and Unknown Possibilities	145
11	Hare Krishna, Hare Rama!	153
12	Right Questioning	171
13	Beyond Polarities, Beyond Time	181
14	Suffering: Broken Harmony	201
15	The Last Luxury	225
	About the Author	237
	OSHO International Meditation Resort	238
	More OSHO Books	240
	For More Information	245

PREFACE

PEOPLE COME TO ME and they say, "We have been meditating for so long. When will it happen?"

I say, "Wait! Soon it will happen."

But these are all lies. If I say that it is not going to happen, ever, you will simply drop the whole effort, you will feel hopeless. So I will go on saying that it is going to happen.

It is happening already, but it is not going to happen in such a way that the journey ends. And one day you yourself will become aware of the beauty of this non-ending process, and you will realize what an ugly question you were asking. You were asking how to end all this. The very question is ugly and absurd. You do not know, but what you are asking is against yourself – because if it ends, you will end with it. If there is no search, nothing to be revealed, nothing to be loved, nothing to be known, nothing to be entered, how can you be? If you were in such a state, you would want to commit suicide.

Bertrand Russell joked somewhere, saying, "I cannot believe in the Hindu conception of liberation, of *moksha*, because in *moksha* – the Hindu conception of liberation – you will be freed of everything. There is nothing to be done, nothing will happen. You will be sitting and sitting and sitting under *bodhi* trees, and nothing will happen because everything has ceased."

Russell says, "That will be too much. It will become a burden, and the liberation will become a new type of bondage. Everyone will get fed up, and everyone will start praying: 'Send us back to the earth – or even to hell. Even hell will be better because there will be something there to be done, there will be some news. But in *moksha* there will be no news, no events, no happenings!' Just think: eternally no happenings, no movement…what type of *moksha* will this be?"

Really, when Hindus talk about this *moksha*, or Jainas talk about this *moksha*, it does not mean that such a *moksha* exists or such a state exists. This is just to help you, because *you* cannot conceive of the eternal process. So they say, "Yes, don't worry. Sooner or later everything will stop, and then you will not have to do anything." But you do not know what type of misery this will be. This will be even more miserable than the earth is already.

Moksha is not a static thing. It is a dynamic process. And *moksha* is not some geographical place. It is a way of looking at things, it is an attitude.

If you can be alive moment to moment, you will never ask when all this is going to finish. The very question shows that you are not alive and you are not enjoying life as it is. If you enjoy life, you will not ask when it is going to end, you will not ask when you are going to be freed of it. Then you are already free. In the very enjoyment the freedom has come. Whether it ends or not is not a concern at all. If it ends it is good. If it doesn't end it is also good. Then you accept it totally.

Osho
The Supreme Doctrine

1

Religion: Knowing through Feeling

Osho,
What is the basic Indian philosophy?

AS FAR AS I AM CONCERNED, I don't see philosophy as Indian or non-Indian. It is not possible. Philosophy is one, universal. There can be no geographical division in the human mind. These divisions, distinctions, are political. Indian, Japanese or German, Eastern or Western – all these divisions are political. They have arisen out of the political mind, but we apply them unnecessarily, and not only unnecessarily, but meaninglessly too in the realm of philosophy.

There is no Indian philosophy as such; there cannot be. Philosophy is an attitude, a universal attitude.

You can see the world through three dimensions. One dimension is science – that is thinking empirically about reality. The second dimension is philosophy: thinking about reality speculatively. And the third dimension is religion: not thinking about reality, but experiencing it.

So science is based on empirical experimentation, observation and objective thinking. Philosophy is based on non-empirical, speculative thinking, subjectively based. Religion transcends both. Religion is neither objective nor subjective. Religion thinks of the whole in terms of the whole. That is why we use the term *holy*. *Holy* means "that which comprehends the whole."

When we call a particular type of mind "the Indian mind,"

RELIGION: KNOWING THROUGH FEELING

when we designate it as such, when we make this distinction, it is not a geographical distinction. When we say *Indian* to me it means that the world, the reality, is being seen neither through science nor through philosophy but through religion. So if you like you can say that this land, this country and the mind that has evolved here, has peeped into reality through religion – not through philosophy, not through science. This third dimension, religion, has been the basis for us.

Reality – when you think about it, any type of thinking is bound to be nothing more than an acquaintance, because when I think about you, I am outside you. I can go around and around, but whatever comes to my knowledge will just be an acquaintance. I cannot penetrate you, I cannot know you from within. So this is just acquaintance.

Science is acquaintance; science is not knowledge. It has to change moment to moment. Every day something new comes; we become more acquainted and science has to change. So science can never be absolute in the sense that philosophy can be. Philosophy is absolute because we are not thinking about the outside but about the inside of humanity, the inside of the human being – the innermost, the subjective core of our minds. Philosophy can be absolute, but philosophy cannot be the whole. The outside has been left out of it.

Science is also a part. Philosophy, too, is a part. Only religion can be the whole, because in religion we are not dividing the objective and the subjective. We are taking the reality as it is – the whole. This whole cannot be thought about; this whole can only be felt. So religion is knowing through feeling.

India has been leaning more and more from thinking toward feeling. The Indian mind – or the Eastern mind – has been non-thinking, non-speculative, non-scientific, and religious. So all religions were born in the East, even Christianity. The West has not given birth to a single religion. All religions were born in the East: Christianity, Islam, Hinduism, Buddhism, Jainism, Sikhism. The Eastern mind has looked through a third dimension. That can be called its basic contribution, but don't call it "Indian."

I am using the term just to make it clear to you. But don't call it "Indian," just call it "religious" – because in the West, too, there have been persons like Eckhart, Bohme, Heidegger, Marcel and Berdayev…there have been persons in the West, too, who were religious. In a way they were Eastern, but born in the West.

There have also been persons in the East who were not religious, who were thinking in terms of science. The first glimpses of science came in China, but they could not be developed in the East because the Eastern mind has become obsessed with the third dimension, the religious. And the West could not develop a religious tradition because the West has become obsessed with the scientific. And, too, there have been persons of a philosophical leaning in both the West and the East.

Now a new world is evolving, a new man is coming out of the historical process – a man of the future who will be neither of the East nor of the West. A new mind is coming into being: a global mind, universal. So we have to discard our obsessions. The East has to discard its obsession with the third dimension, the religious, and the West has to discard its obsession with the first dimension, the empirical, the scientific. And we have to see the world, the reality, through all these three dimensions. Only then, a synthesized knowledge, a knowledge which is total, can be gained through all the doors that are potential to human beings everywhere.

A person becomes whole when he becomes three-dimensional – simultaneously philosophic, religious and scientific. If these three dimensions are simultaneously in the mind, then the mind knows reality through all the doors of perception.

But as you have asked "What is the basis of Indian philosophy?" I will say religion is the basic attitude – the door of feeling, We have used feeling as a means of knowing.

Ordinarily knowing and feeling are two distinct things, but

there are ways of feeling when we *know*, as in love. You can know a person through science, but then you know only the periphery, then you know only the circumference, then you know only the physiology or the chemistry or the biology or the history, but you do not know the person as he actually is. You know about him, but not him. But when you love him, then you don't know the biology, the physiology, the chemistry of the body or the psychology, but you know him as he is – the total. In love, you penetrate to the innermost core, you become one with him. So love, too, becomes a dimension of knowing.

Feeling has been the basis in the East for those who have thought, lived and known. In the West, *logos*, logic – the discursive mind and the analytical intellect – has been the base. For us, the feeling heart, the synthesized mind, has been the base.

But still I will deny the terms "Eastern" or "Western" even though religion has been the predominate note in the Eastern lands.

Osho,
What is the path of religion all about?

Reason is not the path of religion because reason is only partial, and that too, a superficial part of the human personality. Religion needs you as a whole being, totally involved in it.

Reason creates a division. With reason, you can never be total in anything. Religion demands a total involvement; nothing must be left out of it. You must take a jump with your total being into existence. This looks irrational but it is not because even unreason is part of rational thinking. Religion is neither reason nor unreason. It is the totality of your existential being.

So "How to be total?" really means "How to be religious?" – how to act as an organic totality. If not, how can a being be religious? Religion is not a ritual either; ritual again is a fragment. And you cannot be Christians, you cannot be Hindus, you cannot be Mohammedans if you want to be total because again, to be a Hindu or to be a Mohammedan or to be a Christian is to think through reason and conditioning. You can be man only if you are religious.

So a person who wants to be religious must not belong to any religion in particular. This belonging to a particular religion has created an irreligious world. And this belonging to a particular religion makes you very rooted. Then you are not open to all the possibilities, to all the dimensions.

So be religious: don't be Christian, don't be Hindus, don't be Mohammedans. And when you are religious, you will be deeply nearer to Mohammed and to Jesus and to Krishna. Sects are not religion; again, they are rationalizations. So ultimately, religion means a way of life in which your totality is involved. And you cannot be totally involved if you divide the world and existence into two separate and antagonistic blocks.

For example, many so-called religious people have divided existence into two diametrically opposite poles: God and the world, matter and mind, good and evil. These are all rational divisions. A religious being should not allow the reason to divide existence into such categories. Existence is one: matter and mind are one, body and consciousness are one, and the world and the creator are one. If you divide in two, then your life will be a conflict, a constant conflict against something and for something, and then you can never be total. If you divide existence then you are also divided, then your body will become your enemy and then you will be in inner conflict.

And if religion means anything, it means a deep, inner harmony. So I say to you: don't divide; existence is one. The body is nothing but the visible part of your soul, and soul is nothing but the invisible part of your body.

God and the world are not two things, are not diametrically opposite. Godliness is the center of the world; the world is the periphery. Or, you can say that the world is the body and godliness is the soul. Or you can say that the world is the visible part of the divine, and godliness is the invisible part.

Take the whole as a whole organic unity. Don't be against the world, don't be against the body. Be life-affirmative!

So to me, renunciation doesn't mean renouncing the world. It means renouncing the dividing reason, it means renouncing all divisions. One who renounces, one who becomes a *sannyasin*, is a man or a woman who takes the whole existence as one.

If you begin to feel existence as one, then you can take a second jump. Then you can merge with this oneness yourself: the drop dropping into the ocean. Or, even the reverse becomes possible: the ocean dropping into the drop.

Through singing, through dancing, an effort is made toward this merger. When you are singing and dancing, you can forget yourself – still without becoming unconscious. If you can forget yourself without becoming unconscious, you are nearer the jump, the merging. If you can consciously forget yourself, then you are nearer the temple of the divine and then you can enter. At the entrance, only one condition is to be fulfilled, and that is that you must be conscious and, at the same time, "you" must not be.

This is what is meant by meditation: consciousness without any consciousness of the self, consciousness without any consciousness of the ego. All the methods, all the techniques, are basically concerned with this. Forget the self, but remain aware. Drop the self, but remain conscious. If you can be conscious without the self, the door is open.

Jesus has said, "Knock, and the door shall be opened unto you." This is the knock.

2

Discovering Your Own Path

Osho,
People in the West today are crying out for more than theoretical solutions to their human agony. You have spoken to us often about there being 112 major techniques to opening the gates of the divine. Today, from the beginning to the end of this talk, please will you tell us about some of these major methods so that seekers can know and use them?

NO THEORETICAL SOLUTION IS POSSIBLE. Although it always appears that the human problem is a theoretical problem, the problem is always existential, it is never theoretical. It is not a puzzle to be solved by the intellect, rather, it is a river that can be crossed only through an existential leap. And whenever the intellect tries to solve it, it only goes around and around the problem; it never arrives there, it doesn't even touch the problem. The problem remains untouched by the intellect.

Why? – primarily because intellect is the source of creating problems. To be more exact, intellect is the problem. It can never solve, it can only create problems. Just as leaves grow on the trees, problems grow on the mind. It always promises to solve them, but each solution only creates more problems.

Somewhere, Dean Inger has written a sentence: "I cannot love a valid inference. It is valid logically, rationally, but still I cannot love it." No validity can create, can inspire love.

A particular theory can be rational but it cannot inspire you to live it. Validity is of no significance as far as living is concerned.

So the first thing to be understood is: intellect can create problems, can create solutions, but it reaches nowhere. It remains where it was. And life goes on in its own dimension, untouched. By *life* I mean the total being and by *intellect* I mean that part of your being which speculates, which thinks.

If you go deep, then your thinking part is a very nonessential part of your being. Real life goes on without any help from your mind. You are born, you grow, you become a youth, you fall in love, you die. Everything happens below or beyond the mind. The mind is not involved at all in the deeper sources of life.

And every problem comes from the deeper sources. That's why any intellectual approach is irrelevant. Your life comes from somewhere that your mind cannot penetrate. If you ask psychologists they will say that your life is below the mind – your life is unconscious – and the mind is the conscious. And your unconscious is nine times greater than your conscious part. Your conscious part is not functioning for twenty-four hours. The unconscious is functioning twenty-four hours. When you are asleep, the unconscious is functioning. It is regulating everything without you, and more efficiently than when you are present.

That's why sleep is needed so much. The real need is not for sleep itself, it is only for your absence. You must be absent for some time so that your nonvoluntary mechanisms can work unhindered. "You" are a hindrance. With your conscious mind, you are not helping the flow of life; you just create obstacles. So you need to fall totally into the unconscious for one third of your life, otherwise you cannot live.

The unconscious can live without your conscious mind, but your conscious mind cannot live without the unconscious. If you are deprived of sleep even for a single week, you will go mad. And this madness is happening because your conscious mind has been interfering constantly for one week; there was no gap for the unconscious to do the real work of living, the real source work.

And even when you are not asleep, your conscious mind is not working constantly. It is only for the moments that you need it; otherwise the unconscious is working. Really, only in emergency situations is your conscious mind needed. You are on the street and you feel that an accident is going to happen. Only then, for a single moment, your conscious mind works.

So only for moments is your conscious mind needed. Otherwise you are working unconsciously, the whole behavior pattern is unconscious. You may rationalize it, you may justify it, but all justifications are "after justifications" – after the fact, when the thing has happened.

I have fallen in love with someone, then I rationalize why I love. The phenomenon comes first, then comes the whole rationalizing process. Then I say, "Because you are beautiful, because you are so-and-so, I have fallen in love." Afterwards, it appears as if it has been a thinking phenomenon; when you think afterwards, you say, "You are so, therefore I have fallen in love." The real thing is quite the contrary: I have fallen in love unconsciously, and now, consciously, I rationalize it. It is not because you are beautiful that I have fallen in love with you, rather on the contrary, you seem to be beautiful, you appear to be beautiful, because I have fallen in love. Love has come first, then comes the justification.

So not even when you are awake, is your conscious mind working; the unconscious goes on working. What I am trying to point out is this: that the conscious mind is only a security measure, a safety measure. When you are in an emergency, when something dangerous is happening around you – something new in the sense that the unconscious cannot comprehend it, cannot do anything about it… Because the conscious comes from the past, it can only work through the known. Anything unknown, then your conscious mind is needed for a single moment. It is an emergency measure.

This conscious mind tries to solve existential problems, but this it cannot do; this is impossible. It is not meant for this. Of course it can go on speculating, it can verbalize, it can create systems, it can create logical inferences, it can appear to have solved the problem, but the problem remains the same; it has not even been touched.

So the whole agony of the West is basically rooted in this wrong approach. Life should be tackled through living, not through speculation, not through intellectual theorizing. Life should be existentially known. And this is the miracle: if you know life existentially then there is no problem. It is not that existential living solves your problems, rather, when you live life totally, there is no problem. I would like to say that not only does intellect hinder solutions, it creates problems.

Take any problem. If you are in fear – a basic problem, more obvious in the West – what can the mind do about it? Fear is there, death is there. What can the mind do about it? And the problem of fear cripples you totally, it destroys you completely, it uproots you; life becomes impossible. You can only vegetate, the fear will not allow you to live. So what can you do? What can the intellect do about fear?

It can analyze. It can analyze the problem, what fear is. But even if you know what fear is, it makes no difference. You know what fear is: death is there, you are going to end; you exist always on a volcano; never for a single moment can you be at ease. Death is there; analysis cannot do anything at all about it. You can create theories around the problem, but no theory will solve the riddle for you. At the most it can make you adjusted, you can prolong. The fear is there; somehow you can train yourself to neglect it – through theories. But it is there and its working will be there, and its poison will continue to flow in you. It will go on uprooting, it will go on poisoning your sources of life.

There are so many theories to explain, but even if you explain what fear is, it is not explained away, it remains where it was. Theories go on accumulating in the memory and the problem goes on, continuing in your roots of life – and the two never meet. Theories are accumulated in the memory – just a storehouse – and the fear is somewhere underground, in the roots. They never come in contact. Memories can never go deep down into your roots, they just accumulate in a corner of the mind. And they are so nonessential that the mind can be washed completely – your mind can be washed completely – and your life will not be affected. It will go on, unconcerned.

So what can be done existentially? This approach is diametrically different. If there is fear, the intellectual approach is to think about it. The existential approach is to live it. Don't think about it, feel it, live it, tremble in it, let your whole being be in trembling and anguish in it. Don't escape from it, don't postpone it, don't try just to theorize about it and escape from it. Be in it. There is death: one has to face it. There is disease: one has to face it. No one can help you; you alone will have to encounter it.

It will not help at all if you just close your eyes and go on speculating. It will not help at all; it will just create new problems. The fear will be there, death will be there – now you will even fear to open your eyes. A new fear will creep in. You will theorize, explain things, and each explanation will bring new doubts with the mind. The mind will create new doubts and there will be fear, whether the explanation is right or not, whether the theory is correct or not. You will be just pushing the problem back, but it cannot be wiped out.

Live it. The existential approach is to live the problem. Be in it, deeply! If there is fear, then be fearful. Then don't befool yourself by creating some bravery; don't befool yourself that you are not in fear. Don't befool yourself that the soul is immortal so there is no death. Death is there. And you will never know that the soul is immortal unless you know death.

I am not saying that the soul is not immortal. What I am saying is this: that you cannot fool your being like that. You go on saying that the soul is immortal, repeating it continuously, but the fear will still be there. Really, you are repeating it because of the fear. You don't know. You just want to reject the fear through some explanation: "The soul is immortal, so I am not going to die." You can create an illusory, temporary solution, but death is there and the fear will be there.

If death is there, accept it. It is so; it is going to happen. Disease is there: it is so. Old age is there: it is so, it is going to happen. And you cannot help yourself. You just have to face it.

The existential approach means facing life's problems. And once you face a problem, it is no longer there. Only your escape creates it. For example, death is there. If you accept that death is there, it is going to happen, it is a certainty, the only certainty really.

Nothing is as certain as death. Everything is uncertain. Death is the only certainty; it is going to happen. You have been promised death the moment you have accepted life. It is only the other pole of birth, the phenomenon of birth. It is going to happen. In fact, it has happened with your birth. You are bound to die. With this acceptance there will be fear. Accept the fear, accept death – and the moment you have accepted it totally, where is fear?

The fear comes because of nonacceptance: "I should not die! How can I become so death-proof that I am not going to die? How can I be certain that death is not going to come to me? It may come to everyone, but I should be the exception." This creates fear. The being knows that this is impossible: you cannot be the exception. The being knows perfectly well that your explanations will not do, that death will come.

You know perfectly well, you know absolutely, you are certain. As far as your deeper sources of life are concerned, you know that death is going to be. It is not something that is coming to you; it is something that is developing in you, something that is growing in you. So your roots know it well: they are growing death, they are constantly growing. Birth was the first act toward death. Your being knows well that death is there, going to happen. You can befool consciously, you can create theories – and the unconscious will know that you are going to die and the fear will be there.

So don't fight with the unconscious, don't fight with the being. Accept it. Let your conscious mind become cooperative with the unconscious. Don't create a schizoid condition, don't be against yourself. And you cannot be: no one can be against himself, he can only think so. And in the end your minor part, the conscious mind, will know that the major part has won. The major part is the unconscious; your being is the major part.

To me, the existential approach is the only approach. And once you accept this, mysteries begin to open. For example, if you have taken death as part and parcel of life... It is not that life ends with death. Death is the flowering of life – the peak, the ripening, but we create contradictions. We like youth, we don't like old age. In fact, youth is just a preparation for old age, just a preparation for old age. We like life, but we don't like death, and death is just the flowering of life, the peak, the ripening. This contradiction is created by the intellect – speculative, intellectual, theoretical. You can only befool yourself, but you cannot deceive existence, you cannot deceive your being.

So to me – or to Yoga, or to the Eastern approach – the theoretical approach is nonsense. The way is existential and there are so many techniques, but each technique is essentially, centrally, the same. The difference is only of details, The difference is not foundational. It cannot be. The foundation is always the same.

We will take two or three methods that may appear to be contradictory, but the foundation is always the same. One method may be applicable to particular individuals, another may not be. So many techniques exist, not because there are so many ways but only because there are so many individuals. Really, the way is one – it cannot be otherwise – but it has to be applied to so many individuals, and with each individual the details will be different.

One of the basic techniques is that of will. If you can will

DISCOVERING YOUR OWN PATH

absolutely – with not a single wavering of the mind, with not a single part of the mind against it – if you can crystallize your will and be total with it, then you enter existence. There are so many techniques that are techniques of the will. For example, Gurdjieff's techniques for the West were techniques of will. One must crystallize one's will so totally...

Now this is not possible for everyone. For example, the feminine mind cannot comprehend how to be total in will. It is impossible in a way. So those teachers who proposed techniques of will denied women any entrance into *moksha*, salvation.

For example, Mahavira denied it. Mahavira said that women cannot enter *moksha* unless they are first born as men; they cannot enter directly into absolute freedom, into *moksha*. And he has a reason for saying so. It is not because women are inferior – which is what it has been thought that Mahavira was saying. No, it is because they are different. Mahavira's method is basically one of will. It is not the right approach for a woman. And if some woman can succeed in Mahavira's method then she will be a woman in name only. Her total personality will be that of a man, not of woman.

One woman achieved and became a great teacher, of the same rank as Mahavira. One woman, named Mallibai, became a *tirthankara*. Jainas have twenty-four *tirthankaras*, teachers, and one of them is Mallibai. But the tradition will not call her Mallibai. The tradition which says that no woman can enter, calls her Mallinath, not Mallibai. She is virtually a man. Only her physical structure is that of a woman; her psychological structure was that of a man.

Why is this so? – because the whole biological necessity for a woman is that she must surrender. She cannot be aggressive, she must be capable biologically to surrender; she has to receive, she has to be the receiver.

Somewhere, Bernard Shaw has joked about the word *woman*. He says woman means "man with a womb." The capacity to receive, that is the biological necessity. The structure is for that

– the whole body, the whole mind. And if that is not so – if the body is that of a woman and the mind is that of a man – there will be constant conflict, anxiety, anguish, because she cannot be fulfilled unless she becomes a mother and she cannot really become a mother unless she surrenders. So Mahavira's technique, because it is based on will, cannot be used. The whole technique is such that it is a great fight, a struggle.

That is why Mahavira denied any God. He says there is no God. Really, man's mind, the male mind, cannot conceive that there is a God, because if there is a God then he has to surrender; he has to become just like a woman.

You will see the parallel. Those who have loved Krishna, have behaved like *sakhis*, like women lovers. There is a particular sect quite against Mahavira. It is known as *Sakhi Sampradaya* – "women lovers of the divine." It makes no difference that there is only one male – and that is Krishna, "the lord" – and everyone else is just a woman.

But that is the way of surrender. No man can enter through that way. And if someone enters, he will have to be born as a woman or reborn in this very life as a woman.

Let me explain this to you. There is a basic difference, a biological difference, of structure. And when body structure is different, the psychic structure is also different because the body structure is only added to the psychic structure. The psychic structure comes first, then comes the body structure. The body is just a shadow of the psychic structure. It is not that your mind is feminine or not feminine because of your body. Your body is so because of your mind.

So these are two basic biological differences. All the techniques can be divided into two according to whether they require surrender or require will. If they require surrender, then God will be there. If they require will, then there will be no God.

Mahavira denied God absolutely. In fact the Yoga system itself doesn't take God seriously. It can be neglected, neglected because the whole system is based on will. They will not talk about God. In the great books on Yoga somewhere, in a corner, God is mentioned – or even not, and only in later books. The more ancient the book, the less chance there will be any reference to God, because you really only need God in order to surrender – otherwise you don't need him. So the system that takes will as an orientation will make your soul the God. You are the God, no one else.

This is the male attitude toward existence; this is the male attitude. Man, the male attitude, cannot conceive of God as anything other than himself. This is Mahavira's attitude.

But then there is Meera's attitude. It is absolutely different, absolutely. Not only different, but categorically opposite. The will has to be surrendered – that is the method. You should not make your will total; you should make your will absent. It is not that you should be so willful that you can be with your will totally, but there should be no will. You should be just absent, you should not be – and let the God be. You should not be; you should be absent, just absent. Annihilate yourself, surrender.

But still I will say the foundation is the same. What is that foundation which is the same with so categorically opposite methods? The foundation is this: that only one should be there – either you or the other. Two should not be. How you work out which one of the two remains out is up to you. One should remain in the end.

Either there should be no God, only you: "*Aham brahmasmi*, I am God…" There is no other, the will has become absolute, the will has become universal, the will has become cosmic. Now there is no one else. "I am all. I have become the universe. I have denied the other completely." And when you deny the other completely, "you" cannot remain. If there is absolutely no other, how can "you" be? So this is the last assertion of your being: "*Aham brahmasmi*." After that, you will not be – because whom are you against? To whom can you declare this? You have become the total. Now, silence is the only consequence; the only consequence is going to be silence. You cannot even say "I" because "I" is always meaningful against a "thou." It is meaningless if there is no "thou." The male has become absolute.

Then, the ego commits suicide; it cannot remain so absolute. The ego is always in a relationship, it is always against the "thou" or in a relationship with a "thou" so that it can exist. It cannot exist; you have come to a point where only suicide is possible. The "I" will commit suicide because there is no "you" against whom can persist, can go on saying "I" to. That is meaningless now.

And through the other method – the method of surrender, which is quite a contrary method – the same phenomenon happens. You go on denying yourself. A moment comes: you are not. You say, "Only you are, only God is. I am not." This is going to be the last assertion: "I am not" – because if you are not, then you cannot even deny that you are not. This is going to be the last. To say that "I am not" is to believe that "I am." Who is going to assert "I am not"?

So this is the last assertion. Now you will no longer be able to say, "I am not." If you are not then you cannot say: "I am not."

I will tell you a story...

There is a great Sufi, Mulla Nasrudin. He is very fearful of death, as everyone is. Someone has died. He comes home trembling and asks his wife, "Can you tell me how I will know if death comes to me? How can I know? What are the symptoms? How shall I know that death has come?"

His wife says, "You are foolish. You will know. You will become cold…"

Some days afterwards, Mulla is working on his farm. The day is very cold and his hands become cold. He thinks, "Now it looks like I am dying." He thinks what he should do now: "I must behave like a dead man. The body has given the symptoms that I am dead. So what do dead men do? He begins to think, "Dead men lie down," so he just lies down and closes his eyes, because dead men cannot open them.

Then someone passes by. They think that Mulla is dead. It seems so. Mulla wants to say, "I am not dead," but he thinks, "Dead men never speak. Dead men never speak. I have never seen a dead man speak, so it will be absolutely unnatural to speak."

So they carry him to the cemetery. But because they are unfamiliar with that part of the country – they are foreigners, just passing by on the road – when they come to the crossroads they don't know where the cemetery is, where to go. Mulla knows, but he thinks, "Will it be right to tell them the way there? Someone may turn up and then they can ask."

No one turns up. Evening is descending and soon it will be night so they are worried. Mulla thinks, "They are so worried. I must help them," but dead men cannot help.

Night has come, now everywhere is dark. They think: "What to do? We cannot leave this dead body here. We don't know where to go, where his house is or where the cemetery is."

Then Mulla says, "If you don't take it amiss… This is not natural, of course. I am a dead man – I should not speak, the rules don't permit it – but I can show you the way. And then I will stop, then I will stop."

If you are not, then you cannot even say that you are not, that "I am not." It isn't possible. So the last assertion that the technique of surrender will lead to is: "I am not." But that is the last assertion. Only the divine is – and when you are not, how can there be any difference between you and the divine?

When you are not, you are divine. You have reached to the same point through very different approaches: the approach of the will and the approach of the surrender. One kills the other, the other kills your self, but in the end the one remains, the oneness remains.

I have talked about a hundred and twelve techniques. There are a hundred and twelve techniques – different, but if you go deeply, the same. The difference is only of appearance, of structure. And the difference is based not on the technique itself but on the particular person who is going to apply it. One example may make it clear to you.

There are people who are intellectuals – intellectual in the sense that their intellect is more functioning than their emotions. They cannot feel directly. First they will think and then they can feel. Even if they love, they think that they feel love. Thinking must be there; it cannot be dropped. They cannot come to any feeling immediately without the mind. The mind is always there.

There are people who are emotional. They cannot even think without feeling. They must feel first. Even if they are solving a mathematical puzzle they will say, "I feel like this. Do it like this! I feel like this." No reason is given: "I feel that it is like this." Feeling is uppermost.

So those who are intellect-oriented, for them emotional methods will not do, because intellect must go through reason, and emotion must go through faith. Emotion cannot doubt; reason cannot trust. Even if it trusts, it trusts only because it has found that there is no reason to disbelieve. The trust is just a logical conclusion: "I should believe because there is no reason to disbelieve."

With an intellectual person, the trust is negative. It is always negative, it is never positive. It is not that trust has flowered in him; it is just a reasoning process: "Because I cannot disbelieve, because there is no reason to disbelieve, I believe." It is just like a defeat. For the intellectual person to trust is just like a defeat. He feels it, and he will go on trying in so many ways to overcome it. He will create some doubt again, and then he will be at ease. The intellect is always at ease with doubt. It is never at ease with trust.

The emotional person is always at ease with trust and never at ease with doubt. It is inconceivable to doubt. Reason doubts, emotion trusts. So the techniques cannot be the same.

So for an intellectual person, the technique is going to be through doubt, and the technique must be such that it can use doubt. If it cannot use doubt it cannot be applied to an intellectual person: it must use doubt.

For example, in the Middle Ages in Europe, Descartes used doubt as a technique toward faith. He began thinking, "I must not trust unless there is no reason left which can create any doubt. I must go on doubting unless the point comes where I cannot doubt."

So he began doubting – a very arduous process. God cannot be believed in, of course. If you try to believe in God, you cannot believe, because the very effort shows that you are not an emotional person. You first need to have proofs, evidences, witnesses. You must put God in the witness box, only then… God cannot be believed in; there are no proofs, there are no eyewitnesses. And even if there is someone who says, "I have known," he cannot find anyone to witness that he has known. He is alone, so he can be in some deception; he may be deceiving others, or he may have deceived himself. He cannot find any witnesses to say he has known. So God cannot be believed in.

Even the other, whom you are present with, cannot be believed in. Descartes says: "I cannot believe in you because there are dreams in which I see people who are, who absolutely are, and in the morning I find that it was just a dream. Who knows? The night is long, and the dream is lengthy…some day, some morning, I may find that the night is over and the dream is lost."

How can I make a distinction between a "dream you" and you as you are present to me? I cannot make any distinction. While I am dreaming, I believe that the dream is real. In a dream, no one knows that the dream is a dream. Every morning you know that the dream is false, and when you are asleep again, that knowledge is of no use. The dream again deceives you; you take it as reality.

While dreaming you cannot think, "This is a dream." It is a reality. So if my mind can be deceived by dreams in the night, what is the guarantee that with open eyes I am not seeing a dream? Who can make this guarantee – that I am not thinking that you are here? How can I trust that, really, you are here?

So Descartes says, "I cannot believe in anyone else. It may be just a dream, just my thought creation." In this way he goes on doubting everything until everything is destroyed. In the end what remains is only the doubter, and he cannot doubt that – the same problem as with Mulla Nasrudin. In the end he comes to "Only I am." But this cannot be doubted, because even to doubt, this "I" will have to be. If I am to doubt whether I am or not, I have to be. The doubter cannot be doubted. So Descartes said, "This is the only fundamental truth: I can trust that I am."

If one can go through such doubt – it is very arduous, it is very arduous – then you come to the substratum, the foundational truth where doubt is impossible. Then you trust.

So the technique is going to be different. The Buddhist technique, or Krishnamurti's technique, is that of doubt: don't believe, don't believe in anything, go on doubting. If you can go on to the last when only you are…

But even in between, if you begin to believe in Krishnamurti, you have lost the track, because it makes no sense – you cannot believe. If, even for a single moment, you say, "Of course, yes, Krishnamurti is right," you have lost the track; the method is gone. You must go to the end. Not only do other gurus have to be thrown away, but also Krishnamurti; not only do other scriptures have to be thrown away, but also Krishnamurti's writings. With the same doubt, everything should be destroyed.

And, in the end, there will be only you. Not a single fragment of reality is there: no God, no gurus, no scripture, no world, no stars, no suns…nobody else, only you. If doubt can come to this, then doubt becomes a spiritual method. Doubt: you will achieve.

But in one million people not even a single person can doubt in this way, because to doubt absolutely is to create absolute troubles, to doubt absolutely is just to go insane. You have no foothold to stand on, nowhere to have any trust. There is every possibility that you will go insane. That is why only a very giant intellect, an absolute intellect, is capable of going through this method.

It is not that this method was not known. It is not that Krishnamurti is the first one who propounds it. It has always been known, but it has never been of any use to talk about it, for two reasons. One is because among a million people, potentially not a single person is capable of such a doubt. And secondly, one who is capable will not come to listen to you, because the one who is capable of such a doubt will not go to Krishnamurti – he will himself be a Krishnamurti!

Someone went to Mozart and asked him, "I have heard that you have become a great musician without a teacher. So tell me how I can become a great musician without a teacher."

Mozart said, "It will be impossible, because I never went to anybody to ask. You have come to me to ask. If I tell you, I will be your teacher. Go from here! You are not the person who can become a great musician without a teacher. You are not that person. Those who can become, become. If you are to become a great musician you will have to grow through discipline, you will have to be under some guidance, you will have to have a guru – because even this much you cannot understand yourself: how to become a musician without a guru. You have come to ask me! Even this you don't know."

So those who listen to Krishnamurti go on befooling themselves. They are not the people. Had they been, they would never have gone to Krishnamurti. That is the last place where they can go. But they have been going for forty years. Each year, Krishnamurti will come and they will go – the same people. And they have been learning for forty years that there is no guru, that you cannot learn from anyone else. What nonsense!

So this doubt is a method but it is only for the few, so few that it need not be talked about, it is unnecessary. It is unnecessary because it is for so few and for those few it is unnecessary to talk about it: they know it. That's why Krishnamurti's effort has been futile. Whatsoever he says is right, but the fact that he says it is not right. Whatsoever he says is right, but that he says it is not right because it is unnecessary. Those who have come to listen are not the type of people who can doubt. And those who are of that type, will never come.

This method has always existed, and sometimes a buddha emerges.

Another thing: the opposite approach, the method of emotion, is absolutely different, based on contradictory foundations – trust. Doubt it, and the moment you doubt it you are nowhere. The emotions cannot work in doubt. Intellect is the outermost part of your mind. Emotion is deeper. Emotion is your heart which is deeper. Everyone who cannot doubt absolutely should not doubt relatively. If you think you cannot doubt absolutely then don't doubt at all, otherwise you will be nowhere.

The contrary will be easier to understand. If you can't trust absolutely, don't trust at all because no trust can be relative. If you say that you trust with conditions, you don't mean it. Trust is unconditional. If someone comes to me and says, "I believe in you because of this", he has no trust. Trust means that there is no cause. You trust because you can trust. It is not me who is important in trust. It is you. Your heart can trust, therefore you trust. It is not me who is significant. The object of trust is not significant; the heart that trusts is significant.

If you can trust, then trust. If you can doubt, then doubt. The object is meaningless. Go on doubting – with every object.

But decide what type of person you are, otherwise your life will be just a wastage. Decide. Decide whether you can trust absolutely or you can doubt absolutely. If you say, "I can only doubt relatively," you will be nowhere, the technique cannot be used. If you say, "I can only trust relatively," then you will be nowhere, because each technique works only in absoluteness.

This must be understood. Each technique works only in absoluteness. It is not a problem of relativity. That's why every religion has emphasized absoluteness. The reason is not to deny other possibilities; the reason is to emphasize absoluteness. If a Mohammedan says that nothing can be added to the Koran, it is not really to emphasize that nothing can be added, it is only to say, "I trust so absolutely that there is no need." If a Jaina says that Mahavira is all-knowing, a *sarvagya*, it doesn't mean in fact that he know all; it only means, "I trust him so absolutely, that to me, he knows all. Now to me, there is no need to go anywhere else."

Only absoluteness works, otherwise you go on wavering from this to that – sometimes you doubt, sometimes you trust. Then you are just wasting your energies. You are not only wasting them, but creating a contradictory flow in yourself. You go one step ahead and come one step back – and in the end you find that you are where you have always been. You have not progressed, because with each step you negated yourself. If you trust and doubt like this, you are negating your own efforts. If you doubt and trust then you are again negating yourself.

If I speak against Krishnamurti, a person who listens to Krishnamurti will say, "Don't speak against him!" He is not a man who can doubt; he is a man who can trust, so he will even trust Krishnamurti, who is a person who doesn't allow any trust, who is not in favor of faith at all. He will trust him. And where trust is needed, he will doubt. He will go in a temple and say, "How can I believe that this image is of God?" There is no question of how. There are people who can. Do you understand this? There are people who can. That's a question of capacity, not a question of how. And there are people who cannot. That, too, is a question of capacity.

No one is higher or lower. One person is capable of trust; one is capable of doubt. Decide yourself what you are capable of. Then there will be different techniques.

If you go to Gurdjieff, the technique is that of trust. You must trust him. And first he will examine and inquire whether you can trust. He will create such fantastic situations that you cannot believe it. He will create such fantastic situations that you will just escape. If you are a doubter, then he will give you every opportunity to doubt, he will create situations so that you will doubt. Then he knows that "this person is not capable of trust."

Gurdjieff will tell stories about himself. He will create totally false stories about himself. He will put himself in such situations that only someone who can trust, in spite of everything, can trust, otherwise he will run away. Somewhere he will behave in such a rude manner that you cannot stay with him. But if you can stay with him in spite of his rude manners, you will not find a more compassionate, more sympathetic person. But you will have to pass, you will have to pass through. He will always say, "I will not waste my energies, so let me know whether a person is capable of deeper trust."

So there are techniques which are based on faith and there are techniques that are based on doubt, but they both lead to the same. In the end, there comes a point where doubt becomes impossible. In the end, there comes a point where doubt becomes *impossible*: you cannot doubt. That means you have come to trust, even in yourself, but then the trust is absolute because you cannot doubt. The trust is absolute.

Descartes became a very religious person in the end. He came to have such a deep faith that about everything that he had denied before, he said, "It is all nonsense. If I cannot doubt myself, then who am I to doubt the divine?" In the end he said this. He doubted everything and denied everything and came ultimately to himself: this fact could not be denied, this was the ultimate. But then he realized, "If I cannot doubt myself, if I am incapable of doubting even myself, who am I to doubt anything?"

In the end, doubt falls. He became a religious person – through doubt.

Krishnamurti or Buddha – they have also become religious persons through doubt. And the same happens when you go on trusting. To trust means you are annihilating yourself. You cannot assert. The teacher says, "This is night." You know it is the day. If you go to Gurdjieff, he will say, "This is night." The person who trusts will say, "He knows more than me. I have come to learn. If he says this is night, he must mean something." He is annihilating himself. The doubter cannot be there if there is no doubt. The "I" cannot stand if there is trust.

It is surrendering yourself: you are no more. And if you surrender to such an extent that trust is absolute – you are no more – then there is no one who can trust. Then the duality explodes – the truster and the trusted. Then the duality explodes. Maslow says that then an "Aha! Experience" follows. You cannot say anything – an "Aha!" an explosion. There is no one.

The doubter comes to trust all in the end, and the truster comes to nothingness in the end. And in the beginning it appeared quite different; it seemed that the doubter will come to nothingness in the end and the truster will come to everything in the end. But one who trusts is surrendered, he will come to nothingness. And one who doubts is crystallizing. First he will be crystallized, he will remain alone, and then there will be nothing to doubt. When the doubt cannot proceed further, it will have to be left. You have doubted everything, now you cannot doubt. Doubt can exist only in opposition to some belief; it cannot exist in *nihil*. It cannot exist without any belief.

If everything is doubted and there is no belief, you cannot doubt further, so doubt falls. If you have trusted everything, and you cannot doubt further, trust becomes meaningless – because trust is always meaningful against the background of doubt.

The absolute is everything. If doubt becomes absolute there will be an explosion. If faith becomes absolute there will be an explosion. Now, like this, I cannot talk about one hundred and twelve methods, but soon we will discuss them. Each method ultimately leads to the same thing: oneness. Each method is concerned with each particular individual.

In fact, yogic tradition uses *satguru*: the right master. The term *satguru* is used for one who can know the type of individual you are, nothing else.

Each technique is written in the scriptures. You can read them, but you will not be able to know what type of person you really are. The *satguru* is needed only, not to give you the technique – because the technique is written everywhere, you can find it out – but to make you understand what type of person you are. And once your particularity is known, the right technique can be given to you.

To give the right technique is a great science, because each individual differs. Really, there are not two individuals who are alike. Each individual differs; each individual's centers of emphasis are different. Each individual's body centers are different, each individual's body electricity is different, each individual's *kundalini* capacity is different, and has stopped somewhere – where no other individual has stopped. Each one is on the journey, on the path, and each one is somewhere different; no one else is alike. So to know where one is in his spiritual journey…

The method of doubt will not need this. So the method of doubt can deny a guru, can deny scriptures. Only doubt is enough, and it can rely on the fact that those who are not capable will not be capable, will not do it.

But the method of trust will have to make differences. There are differences. Even your type of trust differs. It may be that someone can trust a living teacher. Then you need deeper trust; to trust in a living teacher you need deeper trust. It may be that someone can only trust in a dead teacher. Then you don't need so deep a trust, because you cannot find faults. You cannot find faults with Mahavira now, you cannot find faults with Buddha now. Everything has become absolute.

But with a living teacher… If Mahavira were here, you would find faults. When Mahavira was alive, people found faults – they would find them. It is not significant whether Mahavira has faults – because you can find them, you will find them. If there are no faults and you are a faultfinder then you will fabricate them. You are going to do what you can do, you are going to do it.

So a dead teacher doesn't need any deep trust. That's why the more ancient the teacher, the deeper the trust you feel you can give to him. It is not that you really have a faith. Faith is required only where there is a living person, because each moment he can behave in such a way that there is every possibility you may not believe.

Alan Watts has written of Gurdjieff that he was a scoundrel saint. And it is so, because sometimes he will behave just like a scoundrel. And I say that in that way, he helped so many people because he would just cut you off. Neither your time would be wasted nor his. He would just go.

One day, when he was at Fountainbleu, a journalist came to meet him. He never allowed journalists to come to him, but somehow the journalist came with someone and the friend introduced him to Gurdjieff as a great journalist attached to an international paper.

Gurdjieff asked the fellow who was introducing the journalist, "Which day is it today?"

He said, "Saturday."

Gurdjieff said, "How can it be? Yesterday was Friday so how can Saturday be today? It is impossible!"

The journalist just slipped away, just slipped away! His friend followed him and asked, "Where are you going?"

"Is he mad? He says, 'How is it that Saturday can follow Friday? Yesterday it was just Friday, so how can today be Saturday?'"

The friend came back and asked Gurdjieff, "What nonsense were you talking?"

Gurdjieff said, "If he cannot tolerate this much nonsense, it will be impossible to talk further, because then whatsoever is meaningful to me will be nonsense to him, because there is a realm where sense ends. You may call it "super-sense" but it is nonsense. If he could not tolerate this much, it is better that he has gone. I am a madman, and soon I will say many things that will appear mad to him, insane to him. So it is better to decide whether he can tolerate a madman. If he can tolerate one, then something can be said to him; otherwise, not."

I myself create so many situations. And those who are really authentic, ready to work, will have to pass through them; otherwise they cannot work. The work is in the unknown. The work is that which transcends reason, which transcends sense, which transcends all your understanding.

So if you come with your moral attitudes, your traditional mind attitudes, your so-called knowledge, I will have to shatter it from somewhere. I will have to break it, I will have to make an opening. The opening is always difficult, painful. So I have to create situations.

I create situations. I will spread rumors about myself and will see what happens to you. Someone will say something to you. Then what happens to you? Someone just drops away. It is very good because then he is not wasting my time nor am I wasting his. It is not his path; he must find someone somewhere else. It is good that he drops me. If he remains, if he persists – if he persists in spite of me – only then can something that is beyond, transcendental, be shown to him, be indicated; otherwise it is going to be difficult.

A person who is bound with his commonsense, his so-called sense, cannot, cannot go deep. And deeper are the mysteries. The deeper you go, the deeper the mysteries that will be there – deeper, deeper. You will have to throw away all your commonsense, all your knowing and knowledge. Somewhere on the way you will have to be empty. And only in that emptiness is the flowering.

These one hundred and twelve ways are the most significant ones. It is not that they end with one hundred and twelve. There

DISCOVERING YOUR OWN PATH

can be thousands of methods. Really, each person has to work on a technique with some difference. There can be as many techniques as there are persons. These one hundred and twelve are the basic ones. But this much today – that ultimately they lead to the same. Your differences have to be taken into account.

If you are going to go somewhere, then one technique will do. If you are just speculating, then even one hundred and twelve will not do.

There is a difference between a thinker and a seeker. Whatsoever I am talking about to you is basically arrowed toward a seeker; it is not for a thinker. For a thinker, things will be different. For a seeker, how many ways there are is meaningless. Only this is meaningful: "What way is for me?" It is meaningless what others are working upon. It is only meaningful whether I am working on the way, on the technique that is for me – whether I am working on it.

A seeker is really a scientific mind. He is not only thinking, he has made his own self an experimental field, a laboratory. He is working on himself.

I was talking for ten years, and I saw that people will think about things. But it leads nowhere. Thinking is just absurd – except for the technique of doubt. Otherwise it is absurd.

So now you will not come to hear me speak, now my emphasis is more and more on the seeker. One should be aware of one's particularity, individuality. And once the right technique is known, one should work. And when there is flowering, when there is realization, then you will know that each technique leads to the same, it is basically the same – and of course in details, absolutely different.

Whatsoever technique is given to you, you will only find its validity through experience and through experimenting. And you will be fulfilled, you will be richer through experimenting. Just don't go on thinking about it, otherwise thinking becomes a dead habit, it becomes an obsession. You think about this, then you think about that, then you will need something else to think about, then you will go on thinking about that... Each time you have thought about something you need another object to think about. This becomes obsessive.

With a seeker, this should not be so. So when Gurdjieff wrote a book, All and Everything – this is a one thousand page book – he left nine hundred pages uncut. Only a hundred pages of the introduction were opened. Nine hundred pages were unopened. And there was a note on his first edition to the reader: "Please go through the one hundred page introduction and if you think that you can do something, then cut open the other pages. Otherwise return the book and take your money back. Don't open the other pages!"

There was another note in the first edition: "If you cannot read the one hundred open pages continuously, and become curious about opening other pages first, you are not a seeker and you will not be profited by the book. Don't become curious. Start with the first hundred pages; don't open the other pages. First read the introduction. Only then may you find the book of any help."

Why? Mind is so curious. It is so curious it will not read the open pages, it will first want to read the unopened ones. It will be very arduous to go through a hundred pages. The mind will be working on those unopened pages, will be just going through how to reach those unopened pages. This is the attitude of the thinker. He is curious – hopping and jumping.

A seeker is not like that.

To end I will tell you a story about Bayazid, a Sufi saint – when he was at his guru's school...

For twenty years Bayazid was coming and going to his guru for instruction. Twenty years continuously! And one day, the teacher said, "In the hall from where you are coming, there is a window. And in that window, there are some books. Bring me a book with this name here."

Bayazid said, "I don't know where the window is."

DISCOVERING YOUR OWN PATH

The teacher said, "But you have been coming through that hall continuously for twenty years – every day. Don't you know the window?"

Bayazid said, "I was coming to you. It was unnecessary to look here and there. I do not know. I will go and seek and search."

The guru said, "The book is not needed. I was only asking this to see whether you are a seeker or a thinker. And I know that you are a seeker."

After twenty years he is trying to know whether you are a seeker?

Bayazid said, "This examination – after twenty years? You must have examined me before."

The teacher said, "It would have been too cruel. Even now I was not sure."

The mind is so curious. It is always wandering here and there, everywhere. The wandering mind will not do, it must be focused – insistently focused, intensively focused. It must be narrowed to a point, and only then you can work something out.

Technique means nothing but a method of narrowing down, nothing but a method of narrowing down. Thousands are the possibilities. You must not wander around in them, you must be narrowed down, otherwise you will not be able to work at anything.

Life is short, and the problem is difficult and deep. Your energies are limited. They must not be thrown everywhere. They must be pinned down somewhere. Only then is something possible. Otherwise, thinking just throws your energies everywhere, goes on throwing them everywhere. This throwing of thoughts everywhere and anywhere will not produce anything. That's why a technique is used.

Technique is just pinning you down to a particular, narrow path in which your energies are channeled. Only then can this limited life, this limited time, come to a flowering which is unlimited. Otherwise it is not possible.

THE ETERNAL QUEST

So don't think much. Think only up to the point when you decide. Then begin to work. Then leave thinking. And if you cannot leave thinking, then you don't need a method, you need doubt. Then go on doubting. Then never think about trust; then never think about faith.

But one must be decisive otherwise a life can be wasted. And we waste, we have wasted, so many lives. This is not the first time that we are again wasting our lives. It is an old habit.

Think, up to a limit. When you have come to a decision, then throw thinking away. It is not needed now. Then jump existentially; then don't speculate. Then be in the groove, then be in the flow. And the narrower the passage, the nearer the realization will be. Technique only narrows you.

Now, enough!

3

The Twenty-first Century Approach to Meditation

Osho,
What do you regard as the major differences between the more familiar systems of yoga and the meditations that you have developed?
Is this a fair question?

THERE ARE AS MANY PATHS as there are minds. And each mind requires a particular path and each method is true for a particular person. No method is true as such or false as such. It depends on the person to whom it is to be applied. So yoga is basically individual.

Whenever a society changes, mind changes. We have been devising new methods for the new mind. All the old methods were developed for a particular mind that no longer exists in the world.

For example, Buddhist methods were developed for a particular mind that Buddha was encountering. Now, that mind no longer exists and those methods have become useless. A new mind has come into being. The mind that Buddha was facing and working with was basically based on faith. The whole training of the Indian mind was based on faith; doubt was nowhere allowed.

Now, all over the world, the modern mind is based on doubt, because the whole scientific approach uses doubt as the original source, and a mind cannot be scientific unless it can doubt to

THE TWENTY-FIRST CENTURY APPROACH TO MEDITATION

the very end. Doubt is basic for the scientific approach. Now we have trained all minds in doubt. Those methods that were based on faith have become useless. They cannot be used for the modern mind,.

We have to devise new methods for the modern mind based on doubt, on experimentation, with no basic condition of faith. In each age, new devices are needed. All devices can only be used for a certain time.

My method is more scientific and less religious. It leads to a religious experience, but the method itself is more scientific than religious, more psychological than spiritual, because the modern mind only accepts the body and the mind. The spiritual realm is taken as a romantic fallacy, so you cannot start anything from the spiritual viewpoint; at the most, you can start something from the psychological. So my method is more psychological than spiritual. It leads ultimately to the spiritual dimension but it starts from psychology.

We have been doing much with the human mind, particularly in the West. The religious traditions – Jewish, Christian, Islam and now even Hindu – have all been suppressive, they have been suppressing mind. Now we have layers of suppressions, and unless those layers are released, thrown out, exhaled, nothing can be done toward the inner journey. So my method works with catharsis. The first, basic thing is to go through a catharsis. Unless your repressed mind is released, you cannot proceed further.

Those are the blocks now. They were never there before. Particularly in the East they were never there before. The mind was not so repressive; we accepted things as they were. But now, the whole world lives under a Christian shadow and everything natural has become condemned. The body, sex – all the instincts are condemned.

So we are in an inner conflict. Reason has become supreme and reason has suppressed everything that is not rational. And reason is just a tiny part of the whole being of man – the tenth part, just a small fragment – but this small fragment has become supreme, dictatorial, and it has suppressed everything else in the personality. These suppressed layers have to be released first, and unless they are released and one comes to a deep harmony within – with one's own instincts, nature, body – nothing further can be done.

All the old methods start with you as you are. For example, Mahesh Yogi's Transcendental Meditation starts with you as you are. It gives you a particular technique, a *mantra* to work upon. That *mantra* will help you to calm down but it cannot transform you. It can make you more adjusted to the society which itself is ill, it can make you more still, a certain well-being will come to you, but no transformation – because the repressed layer will remain as it was. It is not even touched by it. You bypass it and you do something with your mind which gives it a superficial tranquility.

All the old methods – if used directly, without catharsis of the mind – will not be of much help. So my method starts with catharsis, and only then, when tensions are released, can you have a deeper jump deep within yourself.

That jump is possible – and I think that it has become so urgent for us, that we can take the jump. But the preparation is bound to be different from how it has always been in the past.

So my method works first as catharsis. Then it tries to create a harmony with your body, because we are living with a gap between us and our bodies. All the old traditions have emphasized that body and mind are two things. That is absolutely wrong. Body and mind are just two poles of one existence. All the old traditions have emphasized that you are not the body. My emphasis is quite the contrary. You are the body. You are more also, you go beyond the body, but you are also the body. And there is no division as such, and no conflict.

But we have created the conflict, and that conflict has created a gap. This gap has to be bridged. My method is a means to bridge the gap, and only when the gap is bridged do you

THE TWENTY-FIRST CENTURY APPROACH TO MEDITATION

become whole. And then the jump becomes possible because you cannot jump as a fragment. One part of you cannot jump ahead of another part. You have to take the jump as a whole being, and to me, *holy* means whole. This wholeness has to be created. So I work on these lines.

The body has many dimensions of its own. If you take it for granted that you are not the body, your body becomes closed, a dead thing hanging over you. Then you are not living in it, just carrying it. So to bring man back to the body is the first thing. Then to bring him to his total mind, the second, and then only is it possible to bring him to his spirit.

So man must first be rooted in the body, then rooted in his natural mind, and only then can he fall down deep into his own depths.

So I am a "yea sayer" – no conflict with anything. And I accept nature in its totality – no condemnation of anything, rather, accepting and transforming.

So I am not very much concerned with old traditions of yoga, not concerned.

> Osho,
> *How do you bring about the catharsis that you are talking about?*

It takes time, but it is not difficult.

How do we suppress? The technique to release the suppression is just the opposite. The method of repression is to not express. If you feel angry, you don't express it. You suppress it, you don't allow it to come out. My method is quite the contrary. If you are angry, express it – not on someone, but in a vacuum. If you are angry at me, don't express it to me, but go into a room and express it in the vacuum – because if you express to someone it creates a chain and you will never be out of it. If you suppress it within, it becomes poisonous. It will remain in your system and will go on doing many, many foolish things with you, and ultimately, you will have to express it somewhere, somehow.

So my method is to express all that is inside. If there are social problems, moral problems, don't express it to people, express it in a vacuum. My method starts with expressing.

In the first step of the technique – we have four steps – in the first step, I insist on chaotic breathing; not systematic breathing, but chaotic breathing, because systematic breathing cannot disturb your suppressed being. Chaotic breathing is very meaningful because breath is associated...it is the link between your body and mind. If you are angry you have a different rhythm of breathing; if you are in love, a different rhythm of breathing; if you are sad, again a different rhythm of breathing; if you are relaxed, a different rhythm of breathing. Whatsoever the state of the mind, the breathing changes immediately. If you change the breathing, the state of mind is affected immediately. You cannot breathe rhythmically and be angry simultaneously. That is impossible. You cannot go into the sex act with very silent breathing. Impossible!

So first I insist on chaotic breathing. That chaotic breathing is just taking breath in and throwing it out, with no yoga system. Inhaling as much as possible then exhaling as much as possible; forgetting everything, just remembering that "I am inhaling and exhaling" so forcibly that every cell of the body is disturbed, and every cell of the mind is disturbed. You are trying to disturb the whole set pattern.

In the second step, when your breathing has disturbed your body/mind completely, I allow you expression. So whatsoever comes to your mind, express it. If you want to scream, scream madly. If you want to weep, weep madly. If you want to laugh, laugh. If you want to jump, be angry, be violent to the sky, then be. Whatsoever you want to express, express – not to someone, just in a vacuum.

So the second step is expression. And you will be surprised

how things start coming to you and you start expressing them – not only with your mind, your body will express them too. For the first time you become aware that your body has many repressions to express. If you are a violent man, your hands will be moving as if you are killing someone or beating someone. Many screams will come out, and with those screams, much will be released.

Only when this second step, expression, is fulfilled… It takes time, but within three weeks you will be expressing very spontaneously and you will feel that something is going out and you are unburdened. Only then can the third step happen. The third step is a particular sound: hoo. Not the word w-h-o, just the sound hoo – meaningless. So you have to do it: "Hoo, hoo, hoo." This hits the sex center inside. There are different sounds, and every sound goes to a different layer within. If you say "Om," the old sound which has been traditionally used, it goes only to the heart. If you say "Om," it never goes below the heart. If you say "Hoo," it goes exactly below the navel and hits the sex center.

Modern mind and modern man and the modern body are so much involved with sex that unless that center is hit, nothing can be done with man. The sex center can be hit in two ways, and that is the source of all energies. Sex is the only energy in you. If it moves out, it becomes biological reproduction. If it moves in, it becomes spiritual transformation – a rebirth for yourself.

In the third step, we just go on crying, screaming, "Hoo!" and hitting the sex center. Soon, within a few weeks, you will start feeling an uprush of energy within, from the sex center to your spine. It begins to move. You can feel the warmth, you can feel that a new path is being broken inside you. And once this energy begins to move from your spine toward the head, you will have a different view of yourself, a different outlook, a different dimension. Once this energy reaches to the head, then I insist that it should be released from the head. Normally we release sex energy from the sex center. That is one pole of our being. The opposite pole is the head. If the sex energy can be released from the head, you are transformed, you are a different being.

So these three steps, and then the fourth step is simple relaxation – just falling dead, not doing anything. Not doing anything: no effort, no technique, just remaining silently with whatsoever is. And after these three steps, you are so exhausted that relaxation comes easily. You want to relax, your whole body wants to relax. You fall down and just lie there like a dead man. In this deadness, you become a witness. You are simply a witness, not doing anything.

If those three step as are done rightly, the fourth follows. And by and by as your catharsis moves further, the second step will decrease. Ultimately it evaporates. Then you need not do the second. When nothing comes to you – no movement of the body, no movement of any emotion – the second step drops. Then the more you go in, the first step will drop by itself – because there is nothing to be disturbed. You go on doing chaotic breathing and nothing is disturbed. The first step drops.

When the first and second have dropped only then can the third be dropped. When you feel that the energy is moving now from the sex center to the head, to the opposite pole, and a moment comes when you completely forget the sex center in your body and your head becomes the center of your being, then the third step can be dropped and then you can move into the fourth any moment, any time.

That fourth is the real meditation. These three are just preparations. And that fourth is just like Zen – not doing anything, no effort; just waiting, silently witnessing whatsoever is.

But it takes time, it takes time – at least three weeks are needed to have the feel, and three months to move in a different world. But that too is not fixed. It differs from individual to individual. If your intensity is very great, it can even happen in three days.

THE TWENTY-FIRST CENTURY APPROACH TO MEDITATION

Osho,
What about the method of just watching the mind?

If you just watch the mind, it will take a very long time – years. And nothing is certain because you are not simply watching: every day, you are creating more mind. And there is a past accumulation in the mind, so it can go on and on; you can go on and on.

I have seen people practicing watching as a method. It is one of the oldest methods – witnessing whatsoever is inside. If you have very little madness inside you then this method will do, but otherwise you can go on watching and it will seem infinite.

Osho,
Isn't it necessary to disidentify yourself with the mind – as if it is outside you?

No, it is not outside you, it is inside. If you say that it is outside then there is no inside and no outside. Then you are part of the universe. But then again, it is inside.

Whatsoever is happening in you is happening in you. You have to throw it out. If you just go on watching, it is possible that meditation may result, but it is a very long process. I have seen people watching for thirty years. They become a little bit silent, but basically the mind continues. The mind seems infinite – you go on creating more of it again and again.

So to me one must first throw out the accumulation and then watch. That throwing out, that catharsis, is miraculous. Then you can relax very easily, then you can witness very easily.

First identifying with your madness, throwing it out, gives you the capacity for non-identifying. If you cannot identify, you cannot disidentify. If you are laughing and you can be totally one with this laugh, you gain the capacity to be totally removed from it. The laugh continues and you can be a witness. If you have not totally identified yourself with your laugh, or your anger, or anything, you are not capable of disidentifying. So this catharsis helps in watching.

The fourth step of Dynamic Meditation is simply to be silent and be a witness. Then these three steps drop by and by. They are not to be followed forever. When you feel that nothing is coming up, the second step drops. But you are not to drop it; you have to continue it. When you feel that nothing is coming up – no anger, no violence, no laughing, no crying – that you have disturbed your bio-energy through fast breathing and still nothing comes up, then – okay. Then the second step has dropped.

When you do the third step, sooner or later it drops. When the energy begins to move by itself, there is no need for hammering. If the energy is moving upward and you go on using "hoo," it disturbs the upward movement. Then you have to drop it. And then you have to drop the first step also, because there is no need. Now only the fourth step remains.

Osho,
For how long should this technique be practiced?

Once a day for forty minutes, once a day in the morning; ten minutes to each step.

Osho,
Is any religious belief required, or can this technique be practiced as a sort of psychotherapy?

No religious belief is required, just do it as a psychotherapy, because as I see it, belief has become impossible. You can only force belief, but you cannot believe. That is not possible now. If you can believe, it is okay, but for ninety-nine percent of people it has become impossible to believe. You can force a belief upon yourself, but that again becomes a repression, so I am against it.

Don't believe. Just take it as an experiment, and start. If something happens, that will become your belief, but no belief is required as a precondition for doing it.

You can conclude with a belief but you cannot start with a belief. And there is no need, there is no need. If a thing is scientific, belief is never a requirement.

> Osho,
> Will the result be transformation?

Yes. There will be transformation; you will be completely a new being, a new birth.

> Osho,
> Will this be a physical or a spiritual transformation?

I don't divide, I don't divide. You are both, and this is for your total being, including the physical. And you cannot have spiritual well-being without having a certain ground of physical well-being. You cannot have.

> Osho,
> So the body and the mind are not separate?

You are the whole: the body is included, the mind is included. But the old traditions of the past have divided you. They have created a false gap, insisting continuously that the body and you are separate. They have created a gap, a psychological gap – not in reality, they cannot create a gap in reality, but they have created the idea in the mind, and now the gap exists. So when I say that a bridge has to be created between you and your body,

I simply mean that this illusion of separation has to be dissolved. You are already one, but psychologically we think of the body as something separate. Totality has to be attained.

So I don't divide body and mind, matter and mind, the world and *moksha*. I don't divide. I say that existence is one. And unless you can feel this oneness, you can never be freed from conflicts, anxiety, anguish.

All anxiety is basically rooted in this division. Because of this division, you cannot live in this moment, here and now. The division goes on creating goals in the future. How to achieve moksha, liberation, salvation in the future? How to be beyond this body in the future? How to be free from the body, and this matter and this world? Always in the future.

Right now, because of this division, you cannot do anything. So first this division has to be dissolved. It is a false division, but it exists. Once the division is dissolved, you are liberated here and now. Then there is no future.

A person who is future-oriented will be sick. He cannot be healthy. The future will go on creating tensions, anxieties.

So there is no future. This moment is enough. If we can be whole in this moment, and live this moment in its totality, it is liberation. And we cannot live this moment in its totality unless we are total. That's why there are techniques – to help you be total.

Look at it in this way. The whole suffering is because of certain wrong attitudes. So reality does not have to be changed, only these wrong attitudes have to be changed. And this is a wrong attitude: to look at the whole in a divided way. It is one whole. But intellect divides, it cannot function without division. Reason divides, it cannot function without division.

So all meditations are basically to give you a glimpse of a non-rational existence where you are not dividing things but taking them in their totality, as they are. I am against division of any sort.

And this is possible.

THE TWENTY-FIRST CENTURY APPROACH TO MEDITATION

Osho,
If your method is purely psychotherapeutic, then why is there an emphasis on dress, why does everyone wear orange?

Because it is psychotherapeutic, because of that: because your mind influences your dress, your mind influences your body, your mind influences your food – everything you are doing. Because it is psychotherapeutic, that's why.

If the method were simply spiritual, there would be no need to change the clothes. What would be the need? But psychotherapy has to look after every trivial thing, because nothing is trivial for the mind. The moment you change clothes, your are a different mind, because something basic has changed.

Dress is not just an ordinary phenomenon. For the mind, it is very significant. The Queen of England is in her dress, in her royal dress…then give her the dress of a poor woman. It is not simply the change of dress, the whole mind will be pulled down. The policeman standing on the road in his uniform is a different man from when he is in civil dress.

Mind is constituted of very ordinary things: food, dress. Everything changes with them.

I give you a different dress, I give you a different name, just to give you a different identity, so you can start afresh. They help, but they are not spiritual, because spirituality has no need to change anything. The moment you become spiritual, there is no need to change anything outwardly. But you are not yet, and everything is going to help you.

If you are wearing very tight clothes it makes you more violent. So we cannot give soldiers loose clothing because if they are given loose robes, like monks wear, they will not be able to fight; the mind inside will become loose. When you are wearing very tight clothes you are more violent and more sexual. If you are wearing very tight clothes your very way of walking is different. You walk in a different way; the pace is different because mind is constituted of very small things, very small things. An ordinary change can be very meaningful for the mind. You cannot stand naked in the street. Why? – because how you dress is very meaningful. It is not simply a question of dress. You can stand naked only when your mind changes.

It helps because it is psychotherapeutic – only because of that. If someone says it is a spiritual thing then that is nonsense. It is psychotherapeutic. And you are constituted of very small things, very small things. If you change them, you change your mind, your past, and you start a new thing, a new nucleus around which something new can be organized.

Take ordinary food. If your food is suddenly changed, your body has to readjust again. You use a particular rhythm of day and night: you sleep for a few hours, you are not asleep for a few hours. If the rhythm is changed your whole body is disturbed.

A new organization is easy. Try this, with very ordinary things. Put on a clown's costume and go around the market, and feel how different you look to yourself, because everyone will be looking at you in a different way now and whatsoever you think about yourself is nothing but others' opinions. If they are changed, you are changed.

But these are psychotherapeutic methods. They help in the beginning.

> *Osho*
> *People try to achieve awareness and higher states of consciousness through drugs. When the drug wears off, they lose this increased awareness. Can the awareness that one attains through meditation also be lost?*

No. once you attain it, it cannot be lost. If it is lost, then your technique was nothing but a drug. And there are drug

THE TWENTY-FIRST CENTURY APPROACH TO MEDITATION

techniques. So this is the criterion: if you achieve something and it is lost, know well that the technique was a trick, a drug.

> Osho,
> Can the awareness be lost even if you don't continually practice the technique?

Even if you don't practice it, once you have come to a point in your being, it can never be lost unless it was simply a dream. Only a dream can be lost.

Drugs cannot give you reality. They can give you a very beautiful dream, or even a horrible dream. It depends on you, the dreamer – you can hypnotize yourself for a particular dream. There are hypnotic techniques. If you use them, then you are in an autohypnosis and you will start feeling things, knowing things. But stop the technique, and the whole thing will disappear. It was just a mental trick; you were playing with dreaming, imagination.

If you really grow then it cannot be lost.

That is the distinction between real methods and false methods. A real method is a growth method, it is not simply a vision. You grow in it; and the vision comes because you have grown to a new state of mind.

With a drugs technique, a false technique, you never grow. A vision simply comes to you, but you remain the same. Then when you are not using the drug or the technique the vision will disappear. It was produced, it was produced chemically; it was not your own growth.

So remember always to grow. Visions are of no use. Even if you "see God" it is meaningless. If you remain the same, then that God is nothing but a by-product of your own imagination. Visions are not meaningful. And drugs have become so prevalent in the West because Christianity has emphasized visions too much – because they can easily create visions. If you are after visions, then I will say: don't go after meditation, that is a waste of time. Then drugs are better. They give you visions easily, but no growth – you remain the same. Or rather, you may even fall down from your ordinary state of mind; you may deteriorate.

With meditation, whatsoever is attained remains with you. Even if you stop the technique, you will not progress further but whatsoever is attained will remain with you. It cannot be lost; a real growth can never be lost. It is not something added to you that you can lose. It is you who has grown.

For example, if you have become a young man you cannot fall back to your childhood again. It is a growth. But if a child is simply dreaming that he has become a young man, he will fall back, he will fall back from his dream.

That is the criterion by which to judge.

4

Hatha Yoga and Hypnosis

Osho,
In traditional yoga, one starts with the body, using hatha yoga methods.
Why is it that you do not teach hatha yoga?

IT IS GOOD TO START WITH THE BODY, it is necessary – but it is not sufficient. There are many problems with hatha yoga particularly for those in the West, because the system of hatha yoga and its related techniques were all developed in a very different milieu for very differently constituted bodies as well as for different minds.

Not only is the mind different today from how it was when these techniques were developed, but the body is also not the same. Everything has become artificial. The whole environment has been so changed by science, that you do not have the same kind of body that people had before. Your body is different. Your mind would not be different unless your body had become different.

When you start with a modern body, the same techniques will not do. Something else has to be added. Hatha yoga can be used beneficially when the body exists in a very natural condition, a very natural, very innocent condition – childlike. Then these techniques are miraculous. But we do not have such innocent bodies now; we have very complex bodies. They are not natural. Changes in the environment have done much to change

HATHA YOGA AND HYPNOSIS

our bodies; medicine has done much. The whole chemical milieu in which we live is different. Even the air is different!

You have a very unnatural body. It is unnatural not only because it has been conditioned by the outside, but also because of too much mental suppression inside. There are very complex suppressions in your body and unless these body complexes are released, hatha yoga will not help or can only help to a certain extent.

Read the work of the German psychologist, Wilhelm Reich. He was a disciple of Freud's. He worked continuously for forty years with the suppressions in the body – not with the mind. For example, he said that if you have suppressed anger then your jaw will be different, it will not be natural. You will have a different jaw; your teeth will be different. Violence is concentrated in the teeth and in the fingers.

When an animal is angry and in a wild mood, his whole energy moves to his teeth and nails. They are his weapons. The same thing happens to man. If you feel anger and do not express it, the energy does not leave the teeth and the nails. There is no mechanism for it to go back; it is a one-way process. When a dog becomes angry he expresses it, but when a man becomes angry he may not express it. The energy that has moved to the teeth and nails cannot go back to where it came from; the chemicals released into the blood cannot go back. They remain in the place they have moved to and tension begins to be accumulated at these particular points in the body. So the first thing that has to be done is for this accumulation in the body to be released.

Hatha yoga does not take this into account, because in former times a suppressed mind and suppressive attitude were not prevalent, particularly in India. In those days, India was one of the least suppressive countries. Now, that is not so. And in the West, Christianity has caused so much suppression that everybody is crippled inside. These suppressions in the body have to be released first, otherwise you start out with a body that is not right, not natural, and many unnecessary problems may be created by it. That is why something totally unknown to hatha yoga has to be introduced now: the body must go through a catharsis first. To bring about this catharsis, a totally new science will be needed, because this suppression is something new.

For example, if you have suppressed sex a lot, then the *kundalini* cannot move up. It is blocked. The whole structure from where the *kundalini* can move up is simply blocked, blocked by the suppressed sexual energy. Or, if you have indulged too much in sex, then you have no energy left to move upward. These are the two problems: either you have a suppressed mind and the energy has become blocked or you have indulged too much so that no energy is left to move within you. You are not in a natural state, your energy is not balanced, it is not a natural flow. That comes from either suppressing or indulging. With balanced energy, hatha yoga can be used very easily, but otherwise it creates problems.

Another thing is that all these hatha yoga techniques were developed for use in monasteries. They are monastic techniques intended for people who are totally involved in them for twenty-four hours a day, not doing anything else. Then too, you have to work with them for a very long period, for years. If hatha yoga is taught to a person who is not totally involved in it – who only comes to do hatha yoga once or twice, or even for an hour a day, but who is involved for twenty-three hours a day in quite a different world, a work that is quite the contrary – it is not going to help much. Whatsoever you have gained is lost every day. The very method is a monastic method.

Now we have to develop methods, non-monastic methods, which will not be undone by the rest of the activities in your life.

This is a problem; this is one of the most significant problems for those who are interested in yoga. In India, people just go on in their traditional way. They have tradition, so they follow it without thinking of whether something has to be changed or something new has to be added The whole world has become

HATHA YOGA AND HYPNOSIS

so different now that hatha yoga techniques are irrelevant in many ways. But they go on being taught because they have become traditional.

India invented many things, but after a certain period the discovering stopped. It happens so many times. Now the same thing is happening in the West, particularly in America. In America, technology has become so developed that now it can change everything. But because the changes are happening so fast, people are beginning to be against technology. Whenever something comes to a peak, it becomes threatening to many of the traditional values and a dialectical process develops in the same society. Many people begin to oppose continued progress. In America, the new generation is moving more and more against technology. If this opposition continues, as it is bound to, technological progress will stop and no further technological discoveries will be made. Then the mind will become static.

The same thing happened in India with yoga. India developed a very subtle technology for inner development; it was an inner science. Once the development came to a peak it became a danger to everything – because if the whole mind of a country becomes concentrated on yoga, everything else is bound to suffer.

India reached a peak of affluence, then it became poor. This was a logical conclusion, because if there is too much concern with the inner world, you are bound to become poor. You are not concerned with outward progress, the whole balance is lost; you become introverted. And once the whole society becomes introverted, outward conditions begin to deteriorate. Because of this inwardness, the whole progress of the country stopped. Then, finally, people began to oppose this over-concern with inwardness.

Since the time of Buddha, India has not discovered anything new in terms of inner growth. Nothing is new since then; it has just been a repetition. And when it comes to bringing these same things to the West, there is a big gap – a tremendous gap.

For the West, many new things have to be done, many new

things have to be conceived of and experimented with. I myself am trying many things. To me, the first thing that is needed is a catharsis. A catharsis releases everything inside you that is wrong, everything that is suppressed inside. You throw out all your suppressions, releasing them. Now, many new things have to be added to the traditional methods. A two thousand year gap is there, and this catharsis, to me, is the most important thing that has to be added. First, your body must go through a renewal.

When something becomes suppressed in the body, you are not aware of it. It goes into the unconscious, it is never conscious. The body is run by the unconscious mind not the conscious mind. The whole mechanism of the body is nonvoluntary.

You cannot feel whether your fingers have accumulated anger in them because if you could feel it, it would be difficult to live. Your fingers would feel so burdened that they would pull you down to earth. There is a natural mechanism that allows you not to feel the suppressed anger in your fingers. You must not feel it, you must forget it is there. It becomes part of the structure of the body, but the mind has no awareness of it.

The mind becomes aware of something in the body only when something has gone wrong. For example, ordinarily you cannot feel that your blood is moving, but if you break a vein and the blood flows out of it, you can feel the movement of the blood. It has only been three hundred years since man has discovered that blood circulates. Before that we did not know that blood circulates because it could not be felt. Circulation is never felt. It is not a conscious thing; the body simply goes on doing it.

The entire body mechanism works unconsciously. You are not conscious of it. Whenever something moves from the mind to the body, it moves from the conscious to the unconscious. The body is unconscious. If you are angry you are conscious of the anger but not conscious of the chemicals that are released into the body. How can you be conscious of it? Whether you

HATHA YOGA AND HYPNOSIS

express your anger or you do not express your anger, you do not know what happens to those chemicals that are released into the blood stream, or to the particular energy that creates aggression. If you have not used it, it must remain somewhere. You develop a complex: the aroused energy becomes a part of your muscular structure, it becomes a part of your body.

Wilhelm Reich had to arrange for two bodyguards when he was treating his patients because when he would push a particular point in the body, the patient would become wild. Many would become so violent that they would attack him without any reason. Reich would be just pushing a person's teeth, and suddenly the person would become angry for no reason. The whole body has so many different points where so many emotions have been suppressed.

In England there was also a man whose techniques are worth reading about. If hatha yoga is to become a modern science now, then the techniques of Wilhelm Reich and this second man, Alexander, will have to be added to it.

Alexander worked with the postures of the body. He discovered that someone has a particular posture because he has a particular mind. If the posture is changed, the mind will change. Or if the mind is changed, the posture will change. The two have a deep association.

In the past, people in India never used chairs. Chairs change your body posture in particular ways. Hatha yoga has no posture to help you if you have been sitting on chairs. It has no techniques to deal with this because chairs were not used in former times. But when you sit in a chair, a certain posture is created and by and by it becomes a fixed part of you. This has to be changed, you have to become more natural, but hatha yoga has no technique to bring about the change.

Western bodies have to be studied in a different way. What you have been doing with your body has to be studied. People in a society that does not prohibit the expression of emotions will have different kinds of postures from people in a suppressive society. In a society where people can weep easily or laugh easily, without inhibitions, the people have a different type of body structure.

When you laugh, it is not simply a laugh, your whole body changes. If the society you have been brought up in has inhibited laughing, then your abdomen will have a different shape than it would have had if you had been brought up in a society that encourages laughter. People brought up in certain societies cannot really laugh because laughter has been inhibited. Their speech is affected by it; everything becomes unnatural, a mannerism. Then you cannot breathe deeply, because if you cannot laugh you cannot take a deep breath. And in the same way, if you cannot weep easily, you cannot breathe easily. Everything in the body is interconnected.

Alexander used to give his patients an exercise called the "Ah! exercise." It was the first exercise he gave to every patient. First one has to relax. Then he has to say, "Ah Ah!" so many times. If you can say "Ah!" the whole system of breathing changes.

In hatha yoga breathing, more emphasis is given to taking the breath in, but Alexander used to put the emphasis on the exhalation. And he is right, because a suppressed mind can easily take breath in but has difficulty in letting go of it, in releasing it.

It is easy for the suppressed mind to take anything in, but to release it is difficult. So a suppressed mind will become constipated in a way. Everything will be taken in and nothing will be thrown out. The body will begin to be greedy, it will begin to accumulate. Even the excreta cannot be thrown out. For this type of mind, the breath cannot be thrown out so easily.

Alexander worked for forty years. He developed a certain technique that is not related to yoga. He did not know anything about yoga – and it is good, because it meant that he had to find out many things through experience and through working with the bodies of Westerners.

In the West, much bodywork has to be done. Alexander and Reich did much to help. Now there are also many sensitivity

HATHA YOGA AND HYPNOSIS

groups working in America, helping to create more sensitivity in the body. It is needed, because Western bodies have become insensitive. You touch and the touch is dead; there is no feeling in it. You can even kiss without kissing, with no inner feeling to it. Sensitivity has been lost, but unless a body is deeply sensitive it is not alive.

The primary thing that has to be done is to make the body alive. So many different things have to be tried, but hatha yoga is not concerned with these things because it was developed for natural, primitive bodies. Primitive bodies are very alive; cultivated bodies are dead.

To be in the body means to be alive. I can use my hand just as an instrument, but then it is dead. I can move my leg as an instrument, but then it is dead. If "I" am not moving inside my leg, then the leg is dead. More sensitivity is needed now, so different postures have to be developed. And first, much catharsis is needed.

Someone was here, an American boy. He came to learn meditation. He had been wandering in and out of many ashrams in India, and then he came here.

I told him, "Meditation cannot be started yet. Between you and meditation, there is a gap. You can go on learning techniques forever, but it will not help because you are not yet at the point where the journey can begin."

So I gave him an exercise. He sat with me and I gave him a pillow and told him to beat it and to do whatever he liked to the pillow.

He said, "This is nonsense!"

I told him, "Do it! Start!"

The first day, he tried. In the beginning he was not very good at it, but by the end he was feeling much. He told me, "It's absurd. In the beginning I had to act, but for the last ten minutes I have been feeling much."

He continued the technique. Within a week, he was as angry

with the pillow as you can imagine. It was so authentic and real. Then on the eighth day, he came with a dagger, though I had not asked him to. He said, "Now the problem is too much! I want to kill the pillow! Unless I kill it, if the anger is not released, I feel so agitated that I'm afraid I may kill somebody. So let me kill this pillow, murder it."

So he murdered it. On the eighth day he murdered the pillow, he completely destroyed it. Then for at least half an hour, he fell into a deep relaxation.

Finally I asked him, "What is your feeling about the pillow?"

He said, "The pillow remained just a pillow for four days. Later on, it became my father. I have not killed the pillow; I have killed my father. It has been a longing in me for three years. Now finally I can go back to my home, to my father. I'm not angry any more. On the contrary, I feel much pity for my father. The violence has disappeared."

Then I said, "Now you can start meditating." And the very first day, he went into deep meditation. Through catharsis, his anger was released. Only then was he ready for meditation.

Everyone is stuck in certain grooves. First, it is necessary to "ungroove" a person, and for this there are many, many methods.

One of the methods that I give people to do is ten minutes of chaotic breathing – as chaotically as possible. Just chaotic breathing: in-out, in-out. Just become a bellows. Forget yourself, do not interfere. Whatever movement happens, allow it. If you begin to strike at the air, then strike. If you begin to scream, then scream. If laughter comes to you, if weeping comes to you, if jumping comes to you, do it. Whatever happens to your mind, whatever you feel, do!

At my meditation camps, I watch people doing chaotic breathing for ten minutes and then allowing spontaneous movements to happen for ten minutes. At least fifty percent or more of the people make movements that are obviously sexual. Anyone can see that their movements are sexual, that it is sexual energy that is moving. Ten minutes of chaotic breathing disturbs the fixed pattern of your personality. Then the unconscious surges up and takes over.

> Osho,
> I am too much in control of my body. My mind is too strong. It would never happen with me.

If you are cooperative, it is very easy. What is the problem? It is the easiest thing in the world if you are cooperative. But if someone is not able to cooperate with his own energy, if he is not able to allow his body suppressions to be released, then he can be hypnotized, and under hypnosis he can be told to allow what is in the unconscious to be expressed. Then, he can begin.

Only rarely can someone not be hypnotized. Only someone who is insane or who is below normal, someone who is not intelligent enough, cannot be hypnotized. You cannot hypnotize a madman; you cannot hypnotize an idiot.

> Osho,
> Isn't the reverse the case? – that a really intelligent person cannot be hypnotized?

A person of lower intelligence cannot be hypnotized; it is impossible. The greater the intelligence, the greater the hypnotize-ability. The more intelligent you are, the higher your I.Q., the more susceptible you are. A genius can be hypnotized very easily, but an idiot cannot be hypnotized at all. Your conception is wrong, but it's a prevalent mistake. What you are saying is wrong, it is absolutely unfounded, there are no grounds for it. But it is a very prevalent concept: that people who can be hypnotized are not intelligent. It is absolutely wrong.

> *Osho,*
> *Isn't it true that no method can work for everyone? I don't think that I could allow myself to let go in the way you are talking about, nor do I believe I could be hypnotized. Isn't the reverse the case, that a really intelligent person cannot be hypnotized?*

If one method does not affect you, another method may. There are hundreds of methods. If one does not work for you then another one can be given or something else can be done. If a person is intelligent and cooperative then it is very easy. On the other hand, if he is intelligent and non-cooperative, then it is a long process. But it is still not difficult, not impossible.

If a person cannot be hypnotized, then his body can be worked with directly, through touch. If you have suppressed anger in your fingers, you have a very different vibration near the fingers. A person who has felt many, many hands can feel in your hand the different vibration that suppressed anger gives to the fingers.

And in the same way, your spine can be felt, all the centers of your body can be felt, the whole body can be felt. Wherever there is suppression it can be felt. It is very subtle – a slight warmth or a slight coldness – but it can be felt. Wilhelm Reich's method was to feel the body. After you have been feeling many bodies you become aware of these things. It is an art. It comes to you; you begin to feel the subtleties.

There are also various esoteric methods. For example, your aura can be studied. It reveals many things about you. Or your dreams can be studied. They also give much information. Or certain situations can be created. Through these situations, you can be studied without your knowing it.

Gurdjieff used to create many situations. You would come into a room and no one would look at you, no one would pay any attention to you. Twenty persons might be sitting there, and they would all behave as if you were not there. You would begin to behave in a certain way which would be studied.

HATHA YOGA AND HYPNOSIS

You are here. A situation can be created in which you are forced to be angry. Then you can be studied. Or, you come in and everyone begins to laugh at you. Suddenly you are a different person. These are situational methods. Gurdjieff was a master at creating situations; that was the way he worked. Study Gurdjieff too. For the last fifty years he has been the most important person in the West as far as yoga is concerned, even though he was not directly concerned with yoga at all. He was trying to do many things through Sufi methods. He would create situations in which your unconscious was suddenly revealed without your knowing it.

Every moment you are revealing your unconscious. I can say certain things about you right now, or at any given moment, because of the way you sit, the way you walk into a room, the way you talk, the way you look. Everything is connected, everything is deeply related.

You say that you cannot be hypnotized. That shows your attitude: a firm, deep attitude. It means much.

But even if I try, nothing happens.

Nothing will happen, because the very trying will be the barrier. In hypnosis, no active cooperation is needed, only passive cooperation. If you are actively cooperative, your very activity will become the barrier. Hypnosis needs a deep passivity, so if you are too concerned with being hypnotized, that will be the barrier, your very effort will be the undoing.

If a person is actively cooperative, different methods have to be used, methods that use active cooperation. That is the problem. Certain methods use non-active cooperation, passivity, and other methods use active cooperation. First, your activity has to be exhausted. You have to be made tired before you can be passive. Then the method works.

But for you, hypnosis can be a deep help, a very deep help.

5

First Freedom, Then Expression

Osho,

One day – it was a Friday when orthodox Jews are busy preparing for the Sabbath – a man who didn't like Jews met an orthodox rabbi on the street. In an attempt to torment him, he asked him to express the entire philosophy of Judaism while he stood on one foot. The rabbi stood on one foot and said, "Do unto others as you would have others do unto you. That is the law. The rest is commentary."

If I were to be met by a tormentor and asked to stand on one foot and explain in one sentence what you have been teaching, would I be anywhere near correct in saying that your teaching is freedom from suppression?

YOU WOULD BE ABSOLUTELY RIGHT, but only negatively. To be freed from suppressions is the negative part, and to express the hidden, the potential – that which you are meant to be – is the positive part. But you are right, because the negative comes first. Unless you are free from suppression, you will not be able to express yourself; you will not be able to achieve your potential.

Society exists at the cost of the individual. It has existed like that up to now. The individual must not be allowed total freedom to express himself. And by this suppression, society creates an image in you which can be exploited.

For example, if the individual becomes totally expressive, you cannot create wars in the world. It is impossible. Suppress the individual, and the suppressed energy that is there can be used for violence, for war, for anything. Once an individual is totally expressive, war becomes impossible. The whole politics and the whole history of man depends on war. The old society has been based on war, and war is possible only if the individual is not allowed to express himself.

This suppressed energy has been used for many reasons, for many causes, for many purposes: for war, for politics, for exploitation. So I am against suppression. I am for natural growth.

I am not against discipline, I am against suppression. Discipline is a very creative thing. Discipline is never against something, it is always for something. For example, I am for the discipline of sexual energies but not for the suppression. These energies must be given a creative turn. But they should not be suppressed. If they are suppressed, then they become perverted. Any suppressed energy becomes perverted and you become less than natural.

Expression means you must become more than natural. But if you cannot become more than natural, then it is better to be natural than to be perverted. The whole culture that has existed all over the world is a perverted culture. That's why it only sometimes happens that a Buddha or a Jesus is born. Otherwise, Buddha and Jesus would be a normal phenomenon, not so exceptional, because when the whole society is perverted, a Buddha becomes something exceptional.

A Buddha is just a flowering of the planet. If the whole society were creative, then *not* to be a Buddha would be a case worth considering, and to be a Buddha would be just a natural, normal thing.

So you are right, you are right. Freedom from suppression and freedom for expression – these two make the whole. Then religion becomes a creative psychology. Then it is not a dogma, not a creed, but a creative instrument.

Of course it is always difficult to put things into one sentence. It is always difficult. But you are right.

THE ETERNAL QUEST

Osho,
Do you recommend any particular discipline besides Dynamic Meditation?

Even to move into an undisciplined life you have to follow some discipline. But you must remain the master; it must not become a slavery. The real thing, the end, is always to be spontaneous.

As we are, we are really conditioned not to be free. Our whole upbringing, our culture, our civilization, our religion, our parents – they have all conditioned our minds not to be free, because a free mind is a dangerous mind. Your freedom is really a deception. You are tethered to a pole. It allows you a little freedom, you can move and say that you are free, but you are still tethered to the pole so you can only move in a circle.

This is man's state of mind. To jump from this state directly into the spontaneous is very difficult. Sometimes it happens, but you need much courage. You require the mind of a gambler, of one who can stake everything for the unknown. Only then you can take a jump.

You can jump immediately from rules to no rules, from your deadened life to the electricity of living, but then you need very deep courage, the courage to lose yourself. But that is rare. When it exists, no discipline is needed, but since it is not ordinarily possible, you have to do something before you are able to take a jump.

You can jump in stages. Then the jump is not so big and you are not afraid of it.

At a certain point, one has to take a jump into the unknown, but before that, certain preliminary steps are helpful. Once you reach a certain point, the jump can happen, but before that there are degrees. It is just like when you are heating water. At a certain point, at a certain degree, it evaporates. But whether that hundred degree point has come or not, heating is helpful. Of course, you can come back even from ninety-nine degrees. You have to reach a certain point before the jump can happen.

FIRST FREEDOM, THEN EXPRESSION

That point differs with each individual. It is not like water, that at a hundred degrees it just evaporates. It is going to be different for each person. It is uncertain. If you could be certain that one particular point was going to be the point from which every individual could take the jump, then mind would be just a machine. But it is not, so the jumping point differs with individuals. For one person it may come on the first step and for someone else it may come on the hundredth. And for someone else, even the first step may not be needed. Each individual has to grope in the dark, but a certain direction can be given. I cannot tell you how many steps you have to take, but I can show you the direction.

Discipline should not be the end, effort should not be the end. The effortless, the undisciplined, the totally free, must be the end. You should never be a slave to any discipline or you will never come to that certain point from which a jump can happen.

Even in a disciplined way of life you can be free. Really, the discipline should be your choice, not something imposed on you. Then you remain the master: any moment you can drop the discipline. And with me, there is no condemnation when you drop it. If you drop it, it is okay. You are free to do it or not to do it; you remain the master. Then discipline is not a discipline. It is just a question of your choice.

Osho,
What makes someone a guru, a spiritual master?

When you are not there, when you have completely disappeared, the other becomes an open book to you. The more other-oriented you are, the less you can know what is happening to the other. The more you become self-oriented, the more possibility there is of knowing what is happening within someone else. A moment comes when you are completely dissolved. Then you know the other totally. Then the other is not the other; he is not something separate from you. You don't react to him; there is no need. There is a response, not a reaction. Only in this way can one become a guru and help others, otherwise not.

To me, a spiritual master needs this capacity of being totally uninvolved, of being totally unrelated – just being an absence, with nothing to impose, nothing to project, no need to react. Then he can help you. He cannot come to any conclusions about you; he just responds to you.

That is what being with a guru means: being with a person who doesn't react. Just by being near him you become more and more aware of yourself, if you are really a disciple. And by being a disciple, I mean being open to the presence of the master. You may be sitting before a mirror with closed eyes. Then the mirror cannot show you anything. The mirror is a mirror because it does not do anything on its own. It is a non-doer; it is only a presence. It cannot do anything positive.

The moment you begin to do something positive with someone, you become disturbed. You begin to change your form, you become violent. Even to do good is a violence, a subtle violence. If I don't accept you as you are, I have to cut you somewhere, destroy something, change you like a sculpture, break you. Some pieces have to be thrown away, something has to be rejected; I will hammer you. It is violence, a very subtle violence – the violence of the good man, the moralist, the religious man.

A real master will not even try to make you good. Only then is he a master. He is mirrorlike, just a deep absence.

But you cannot be helped by the mirror, by the "no one," by the nothingness, if you are closed. You can sit with closed eyes, but then for you there is no mirror at all.

By being a disciple I don't mean being a follower – no. A follower, again, is someone violent – violent against himself. He is in need of someone who can be violent with him. He is a masochist. He wants someone to cut him, to change him, destroy him, transform him. He is a follower. He says, "Give me a discipline, give me the way. Tell me, order me, and I will obey." He is really in search of some slavery.

Osho,
But maybe some people need slavery?

No one needs slavery. One may want it, but wants are not always needs. You want slavery because the moment you become a slave, you are completely without responsibility. You are free in a way; a slave is free in a way. Now, he is not responsible.

Even if he does something wrong, the master will be responsible: "I am following you. If I have not reached, you are responsible. I have obeyed you." Now the master is going to be guilty, not him. He says, "I surrender completely." This is not surrender! Really, it is something criminal. He is trying to say, "Now, from this time on, I will never be guilty again. You are going to be guilty. If I do not reach the divine, you are responsible; you will have to answer for it. I have surrendered myself to you." That's why he wants to be a slave.

But slavery is not a need. You can never be free from responsibility. The more you are freed from it, the less conscious you become. You can become freed from responsibilities only when you become an automaton, a machine, a mechanical device. So followers become machinelike. The more they follow, the more machinelike they become.

This is not really the need. It is not a growth. But this is what many people want. You want to throw the responsibility, the burden, on someone else. And really, a person who is throwing away his responsibility can never be free.

Osho,
My fear has been that if I follow your methods of meditation, I will be leaving my responsibilities.

THE ETERNAL QUEST

You are not going to leave your responsibilities, rather you are going to add some new responsibilities. Doing this meditation is going to make you more responsible. You are going to become more free, and a free individual is responsible. You are taking the whole burden for your growth on yourself; you are not throwing the burden on me. You are not becoming my follower, you are not following me.

I am not promising you anything. But by following my suggestions, you may achieve something. I am saying that by doing such and such a thing, you will grow. That is not following me. By doing something you may gain much, but the whole responsibility remains with you. I am not going to feel responsible for you or anyone else. If you fall, you fall. If you rise, you rise. When you achieve something, you need not even be thankful to me; you can just forget me. That is the only thankfulness that can be given. If you have to be thankful to me when something is achieved then "the other" will be there. Then, if you don't achieve anything, I am responsible.

You are not to follow me – really. The very word *follow* is not good. To be a disciple is not to be a follower. To be a disciple only means to learn: to learn, to be a learner, to be a receiver – not to be a follower, because a follower can never learn. Before he learns, he begins to follow. A follower means that you have decided that the other person is right "...and I have to follow him." The decision to follow has come first.

A disciple is something quite different. He is not a follower, he is a learner. He has come to learn. He has come to no conclusions. With a conclusion, you become closed. Then you just close your eyes and follow me.

To follow someone you have to close your eyes, otherwise every moment there will be doubts, every moment there will be something that you can't follow. So a follower has to be really blind. A blind follower is the only follower, the only bona fide follower. If your eyes are open, you cannot be a follower.

By *disciple* I mean a learner, and by *learner* I mean one who is

FIRST FREEDOM, THEN EXPRESSION

open, one who is without enclosures, one who is ready to inquire. This opening creates receptivity and makes you a disciple. If you are near a mirror with this open consciousness, many things will begin to happen without any discipline being imposed. Neither the master is trying to change you nor are you trying to change yourself.

Just by having an open mind and being with a mirrorlike man, things will begin to happen. They go on happening and much is transformed, much is changed without any effort to change it. This is what the Indian term *satsang* means. The word means "in communion with truth" – in communion with someone who has become the truth.

> Osho,
> What you talk about can mean so much to so many people. Your message has to spread, it has to bring about a spiritual explosion. That seems to be the only hope there is for us today. How do you intend to let your ideas grow and spread and blossom; flower into something more universal, more accepted, more usual?

This is a very difficult question. Difficult because, as I see it, the moment you begin to organize a thing, it begins to die. The moment you begin to propagate a thing, it becomes a dead dogma. The moment you say that everyone should live according to this, you become a very great enemy – with good, warm wishes!

So as far as I am concerned, I just go on living the way I feel is right. I go on saying whatsoever I feel is right without any intention of making the whole world be in accord with it – with no plan. In that way I am an anarchist. I don't think any religious person can be otherwise.

The moment a religious person is followed by a group who can plan, the whole thing becomes not only nonreligious but, ultimately, antireligious. This has always happened. Every religion has done this, and no religious person has ever intended this to happen. So this has become a necessary evil. Whenever there is someone who has something to say and who has something to show, how it should be propagated to everyone comes very easily to our minds. And this is good, and this is done with compassion. But the very nature of things is such that the moment you begin to organize, to propagate, it becomes a mission. The thing for which you were trying dies in the very process. This is the very nature of things, and you cannot do anything about it.

So for me, more religious people are needed in the future, not religious organizations. Unless we discard organizations, the explosion we are talking about will never come. That explosion cannot be brought, it can only come – and we can help it to come by not organizing according to ideologies. Every ideology is good when it begins. Then, by and by, it has to compromise, to compromise for the sake of the organization.

That is what I was saying today. It is very difficult and very miraculous, but sooner or later the means become the end. You begin to organize for an ideology, and then ultimately the ideology begins to exist just for the organization. The organization becomes more important, and you have to compromise for the organization. Ultimately, the idea dies and only a church remains.

And there are so many churches that no new church is needed. I am against churches. Really, I am against the very spirit of a missionary. As I see it, if I begin to be too much concerned with your change, I begin to be violent. If I am too concerned with changing you anyhow, with making you good, then I begin to be violent. And the violence that happens with good intentions is more dangerous than ordinary violence. All your so-called *mahatmas* are very violent people. They will not allow you to be yourself.

So what am I to do? It is a problem. I feel that something can be done, I feel that much is needed to be done, but it must be done in such a way that, in doing it, the quality of the thing is not going to change. And if the quality changes, then I am for the quality, not for the doing.

So I will go on talking. This talking is more or less individual. Even if something has to be done, it is just functional, utilitarian. I must behave not like a missionary, but like a poet. A missionary is more concerned with you and your change. A poet is more concerned with himself and his expression. If something happens in you, that is not the point. I must say what is right as it looks to me. If something happens in you, it is okay. If nothing happens, it is also okay. I have told it as best as I can. It is enough; I must not be concerned with the result.

In a way, too much concern with the result is what is known as a worldly mind. Why should I be concerned with the result? I have spoken, I have lived. If you feel something is valuable, you can choose it. This choice must be yours. It must not be enforced in any way; it must not be manipulated in any way, you must not be convinced by it. No conversion is good.

So you can choose. And this choice will be more alive because you choose it, you remain in yourself. It becomes a part of your greater unity. It is bound to undergo a deep change. In you, it will be a different flowering. But if I force it upon you then it will just be an imitation. Then you will be just a follower, not an authentic being. And followers are not good, not good at all. They are dangerous people!

So what can I do? I can do only one thing: I can communicate. And if I am not concerned with your conversion, then communication is easy, communication is heart-to-heart. But if at any moment you feel that I am concerned with changing you, you will become defensive. Then I will have to fight. Then it is a fight, not a communion.

So I will not organize, because the only spiritual explosion in the world will have to be through individuals and not through organizations. All organizations have failed – political, religious, social. All organizations have failed. And really, the mess the

THE ETERNAL QUEST

world is in is because of these organizations. Every organization was created around a very good idea, a very good, alive thing. It may be a Buddha or a Zarathustra or a Jesus – a very alive person with something revolutionary, something essential to impart. But then...

You must have read a story by Leo Tolstoy. In it, he creates the parable of Jesus coming back after fourteen hundred years to see how the world has progressed under Christianity: "This is the time for me to be welcomed. When I was here before, there was not a single Christian. That is why I was crucified. The crucifixion was because there were no Christians. Now I will be as welcome as anything. Half the world is Christian!"

So he comes. He comes to Bethlehem on a Sunday. People are coming out of church. He stands under a tree, and he feels that everyone will recognize him – they are coming from *his* church. But people begin to laugh and make jokes and they say, "You are acting very well – just like Jesus."

Jesus says, "I am not acting. I am the real Jesus!" They begin to laugh even more.

Then somebody says, "Whether you are real or not, escape from this place, because the High Priest is going to come out soon and you will be in real trouble."

Jesus says, "But he is my priest. Even if you do not recognize me, he must recognize me." So Jesus waits.

Then the High Priest comes. He looks at Jesus and says to the crowd, "Bring this man to the church. He is trying to create a nuisance. Either he is mad or just trying to create some trouble."

So he locks Jesus in a room. Jesus feels very disturbed. Again, the whole thing begins to take the same shape. It looks as though the world has not changed at all, and the Christians are behaving in the same way as the non-Christians have done. But he waits.

At midnight, the priest comes, unlocks the door falls down at Jesus' feet and says, "I have recognized you. You are Jesus. But

I cannot recognize you in the marketplace; in the crowd I cannot recognize you. I could not recognize you because you are the old disturber – the old disturber! You will destroy everything, and we have put everything right; now we have organized the whole thing. And if you are back again, you will destroy everything. So please, we are working very well. You are not needed at all. Be with your father in heaven. We are your representatives here; we will take care of everything. We will take every care; you are not needed.

"And I am saying this to you privately. Please don't quote it anywhere because then I will be in trouble. And you cannot be otherwise; you are an anarchist. So it is not that you were against the Jews, it is not that you were against the Jewish church. You are against the church, you are against organization, and you are against everything that we stand for."

And this is authentic in a way; and the priest is right. Whenever we organize, the whole mechanism of organization is such that a church comes out of it, not a religion. And once a church is there, it is always against religion. Any church is against religion. And it cannot be otherwise, because *religion* means rebellion, *religion* means individuality, *religion* means freedom. The church cannot mean these things. The church must mean something else: a deep slavery, a spiritual slavery, a following, a dead dogma, a creed, a routine ritual. And *church* can never mean freedom because a church cannot stand with freedom.

But this has always been so. And now I think that the human mind, and human consciousness, and human history have come to a point where we can begin to be individually religious. No need to be a Jew, no need to be a Hindu or a Christian – just being religious must be enough. That means religion must be freed from all social phenomena. It must become an individual existence.

So what can I do if this is in my mind? How can I go on communicating? – not waiting for results at all, not waiting for any continuation of my thought, not working so that it will be there for centuries...

It should not be. Really, this is a very wrong conception. Why should it be? A flower has flowered. By the evening, it must die, just like that. Any idea that has flowered must die. It must not try to be permanent. It must allow other flowers to flower; it must die so that tomorrow something else can flower. If I create an organization, then I kill the chance for something else, something new to come up tomorrow.

So I am not intending anything at all. There is no planning, no future; this moment is enough. And even if our communication can make something happen in one single individual, then it is worth everything, it is worth the whole earth.

It can happen, but it must be a chain reaction. And we must be patient. A missionary is never patient, can never be. Otherwise, he cannot be a missionary.

Osho,
What is neo-sannyas all about?

Neo-sannyas is an effort to introduce the concept of *sannyas* without any renunciation of the world.

To me, India has given only one thing to the world, to human consciousness, and that is the concept of *sannyas,* the concept of renunciation. But this renouncing can be one of two things.

It can be of the world. Then it becomes negative, it becomes life denying, it goes against life.

To me that negative, life-denying aspect of *sannyas* is a disease. And because of that life-denying aspect, *sannyas,* religion, has suffered much. It couldn't become a major part of life, it couldn't become a part of human consciousness. The main current of it is life denying.

Neo-sannyas is a total yes to everything in life – including everything that gives you higher consciousness, including everything that gives you a nearness to the divine, including everything that has been denied only because it was life-affirming, for example, love.

Neo-sannyas accepts life in its totality, and also sex in its totality – but not drugs, because drugs are an effort to be more and more unconscious, to be chemically seduced into a deep lethargy. Anything that helps consciousness, anything that makes you more alert toward the reality is included.

Osho,
Is it a mingling of different religious concepts?

It is not a mingling. Rather, it is the essential foundation of all religions. It is not a compromise of all the religions. Rather, on the contrary, it is the essence of all religion.

When a Jesus achieves something, the outward behavior, the outward ritual that evolves around him, becomes Christianity. But the innermost core is lost. When a Buddha achieves something the same thing happens. The unknown is achieved again, but the nonessential begins to be more important, and Buddhism is created.

So neo-sannyas is not a mingling of Buddhism and Christianity and other religions, rather, it is a reassertion of the essentials that make a Buddha a Buddha and a Jesus a Jesus. And that essential is one. So I say yes to all religions as religions, and no to all religions as sects.

Osho,
What is your attitude toward sex, and sex outside of marriage?

Sex is very important because sex is the root of life. You are born out of sex, your every cell in the body is a sex cell. Sex cannot be denied and any society that denies sex becomes suicidal. Then it is denying life itself.

So sex is very significant, very meaningful. But you can do two wrong things with sex. One is, you can be suppressive. Then, you create perversions. In the West, Christianity has created a very perverted mind through too much of a "no attitude" toward sex, too much fear about sex. Too much suppression has created a reaction. That suppression will lead to perverted mind. So I am not for suppression. Nor am I for indulgence. Indulgence is again a reaction. Indulgence is the opposite extreme to suppression. That, too, is not good.

I am for healthy sex that is neither indulgence nor suppression. Sex must be accepted in its totality. Then the question of inside or outside of marriage is irrelevant, because marriage is just a part of the social system; there is nothing natural about it. To me, to be really authentic in your sex life you have to go beyond the structure of marriage.

You become inauthentic in two ways. If someone is in a sexual relationship with someone that he or she doesn't love, to me it is immoral, even if he or she is one's husband or one's wife. If one is not in love then it is immoral. If love is the base, only then can you be honest, sincere and authentic. If love is the base then marriage becomes, by and by, a superficial structure.

> *Osho,*
> *What is your view of pornography and what are your views on the new morality of sexually free societies like Sweden?*

I will not condemn. I appreciate it. Sexually free societies are not degraded, rather, they have come to face the facts of life honestly. They are more honest than so-called moral societies, which are basically dishonest. If sex is a fact then you must take it as a fact – no beating around the bush.

FIRST FREEDOM, THEN EXPRESSION

And pornography is an art, unless your mind is perverted. If your mind is perverted, pornography becomes a disease. Otherwise it is a simple art. If I paint a beautiful flower you appreciate it, so why not appreciate it if I paint a nude woman? It is just as beautiful. And if a naked flower is beautiful, a naked woman or a naked man is also beautiful.

But a naked flower will not create any attitude in you of condemnation, whereas a picture of a naked woman will – not because it is pornography, but because the whole culture bas been anti-sexual.

Sweden is really the vanguard of the new morality that is developing. It is not a degraded society.

Osho,
Do you consider India hypocritical in this respect?

Yes. Now, it is a country of hypocrites.

Whenever a country reaches to the peak, to the flowering – when it is healthy and young, fearless of everything – then truth can be taken as truth. In India's golden days we created Khajuraho, Konark, Puri. It was rare, daring. There is no comparison to them, not only in India but in the whole world. A temple of God that has sculptures of *maithun,* of sexual intercourse – there is no pornographic attitude toward sexual intercourse; it is so meditative, so celestial.

But those were the days when the country was healthy, young; taking life as it was, celebrating life in its totality.

Today it is a dying country, an old country just struggling to be alive somehow. The India that exists today must die, in a way, in order to be reborn. Only then will hypocrisy go. A very old man becomes a hypocrite.

For the first time in the world, Eros – sex and love – is becoming more significant. It is the antidote to war. If sex is suppressed then you become violent. Really, wars are nothing but a by-product of suppressed sexuality, suppressed sex energy. Regardless of how much they talk about peace, your politicians, your so-called moralists are creators of wars.

Now – and it is really for the first time in the world – the younger generation is for love, for sex, for life. This is a very optimistic possibility. With these young people, a different world is going to be born.

If we emphasize love and life more, no one will be ready to fight. It is really a question of choosing between Eros and death. "Make love not war" – it is very symbolic. Make love and then you cannot make war. But if you cannot make love, you cannot make anything except war because the very energy that can love and create becomes perverted.

Love is creative. If there is no love, then that same energy becomes destructive.

Osho,
Is love our basic energy?

It is practically love, but not just that.

I call the name of the basic energy, the energy that we are, *life*. If life becomes love, inner growth is happening. Then love can become light – that is another growth.

If life becomes love you are on the path, and if love becomes light you have reached.

These three words are very meaningful to me: *life*, the basic energy, *love*, the transformation of this energy into a celebration, and *light*, the transformation of love – through meditation – into divine existence.

Osho,
When I go back to my own country, what plan should I follow in trying to teach your methods to others?

FIRST FREEDOM, THEN EXPRESSION

Do not plan anything. Just go on digging within yourself. Things will take their own course.

Planning always presupposes frustration. When you plan, you create the seeds of frustration. Do not plan, just go on working. Let it come. It is always beautiful when it comes by itself. It is always fulfilling, never frustrating, because there has been no expectation. And when there is no expectation, you are never disappointed. The less you are disheartened, the more you can do. The more you are disheartened, the less you do.

So I say again: do not plan. Just go on. Let it come by itself. When we plan, we hinder the way of its coming. Because of the plans we make, life cannot work. Our plans get in the way.

I lead my life with no plans and I have never been frustrated. There is no question of frustration, so I am always successful. I cannot be a failure because there is no plan against which I calculate.

No failure is a failure, no success is a success. Only our conceptions and predetermined plans make them so. If you fail in your plan, you feel disappointed; the ego is hurt. If you succeed, the ego is strengthened and it will plan more, ceaselessly, causing perpetual strain and burden on the mind. The ego is always afraid of life. In life we never know what is going to happen so we make plans for our security. But life continually disturbs our plans because we are not the whole and soul of life; we are only a negligibly small part of the infinite existence.

The moment you start planning, you begin to compare and contrast. Doubts and fears catch hold of you. Will I succeed? Is it possible? What will happen? What will people say? The moment you plan, the seeds of frustration take root. Now the anxiety will follow. We make plans in order to be free from anxiety, but the plan itself creates anxiety. We become anxious because of our plans, our expectations

So do not plan, just go on. You do not plan your breathing, you just go on breathing! Let it come to you easily. All that comes easily becomes divine and nothing that comes with effort can be divine. The divine comes effortlessly. It is, in fact, coming all the time. Let it come. Just let go of yourself and see. Things will begin to move. You will find yourself in the midst of movement, but there will be no anxiety, then there will not be any trouble created for the mind. If something happens, it is all right. If nothing happens, then too it is all right. Everything is all right with a mind that does not plan, that accepts life as it is. Only then can meditation happen, otherwise not.

Meditation is not a business. It should not be made a business. If it is, you will not be able to help others toward meditation, much less yourself. Rather, you will be suicidal to your own meditation because it will be a burden to you.

If meditation has come to you, if something has flowered in you, the perfume will spread. It will work in its own way. Something has happened to you. You are calm and at ease, tranquility has been achieved. That will do the work; you will not have to work. What has happened to you will draw people to you. They will come by themselves, they will ask about what has happened to you.

Let others plan. You, just go and meditate. Things will begin to happen, they must happen. Only then do they have a beauty of their own, otherwise not.

Business is always tiring. It has no beauty, no joy. Meditation is not a business but it has been converted into a business in India – a flourishing business. There are shops and there are factories. Do not take meditation in this way. You have experienced meditation, you have come to the door. You have seen something, you have felt something. Let it go on – let existence work.

When you leave here, go completely without planning. Do not even plan not to plan or it will be the same thing. Don't think at all about what you are going to do when you return home. Just be there. Your very presence will begin to work. Only then will it be my work. If you plan, then it will not be my work at all. You will be merely distracting yourself and others. You cannot help others to meditate if you yourself are tense. You cannot help them. You will be helpful only if you proceed without plans.

Just go. Sit there, meditate and see what happens. Things are bound to take their own course.

6

Consciousness:
Living in a Vertical Dimension

Osho,
Many Western historians feel that humanity is constantly making progress. If this is the case, then how is it that human consciousness is so unevolved?

THE PROGRESS OF HUMANITY and the progress of human consciousness are two quite different dimensions. The progress of history is in time and the progress of consciousness is not in time. The progress of all that we can see, of all that is visible, is horizontal, while the progress of consciousness – which we cannot see – is vertical. And we cannot see it because it is vertical.

That is why history can never be in tune with the evolution of the human mind. At the most, it can deal with the outward form; it can never get to the spirit. But that is not the fault of history, or of historians, or of the way in which history is written. Such is the nature of things. History can never be in contact with the formless; it can only talk about the form.

The formless is always transcendental to history, and the real evolution is always formless. Outward progress is not really evolution, it is simply accumulation. There is no qualitative mutation in it; the change is only quantitative.

History can never transcend time. It can know only about those events which occur in time. It cannot know something that occurs beyond time, that is, non-temporal. Events can be perceived through the historian's eye: events exist at a

CONSCIOUSNESS: LIVING IN A VERTICAL DIRECTION

cross-point between time and space. An event happens somewhere, at some time. So the questions *where* and *when* can be asked about events – it will be relevant – but where and when cannot be asked about spiritual happenings. There, time and space are both irrelevant.

For example, Gautam Buddha achieved realization. He jumped into the absolute. He knew and realized all that can be known and realized. But when did it happen – and where?

History will ask *where* and *when*. The event has occurred, so we can fix the point, we can know the date, time and place. But even if we know at exactly what time and at what place this happening occurred, we do not have the fact itself. What has occurred remains transcendental. Where it has occurred we can know, when it has occurred we can know. But what has occurred to Buddha, what has happened within him?

History will say that under the *bodhi* tree – at this time and at this place – Gautam became enlightened, became a buddha. But what is this happening, this Gautam becoming a buddha? What has happened to him? The happening transcends history completely. And that happening is the real evolution of the human mind.

The nature of things is such: History is not at fault, it cannot go beyond time, it has a limitation, it is a temporal record. When a spiritual happening comes to exist, it touches time but is never within time. It happens somewhere, but the time and place are irrelevant. Whether Buddha was under the *bodhi* tree or not is meaningless. It has nothing to do with the phenomenon that has happened in him. Whether the *bodhi* tree exists or not, whether Gautam was in India or Palestine, it makes no difference; when he became a buddha, he jumped into nowhere-ness. The phenomenon itself is not at all concerned with time and space. Once he is a buddha he is nowhere – neither in time nor in space. He jumps out of the realm of history.

That is why we have never been concerned with history in India. We concern ourselves only with that which is meaningful.

THE ETERNAL QUEST

Concern with death is beyond history, all that is meaningful is beyond history, so history became meaningless to us. It records all that is nonsense. So India, the Indian mind, became non-historic. It is only with Christianity that history became meaningful.

History became meaningful with Christianity because a time concept, a linear time concept, came into existence. If time progresses linearly, if time progresses in a line, no event is repeatable. History cannot repeat itself because the past goes out of existence. The line is always going forward.

The Indian concept of time is circular. It does not progress in a line. It is always circular, coming back to itself. That is why, in India, the wheel symbolizes time. The wheel of the Indian flag is the Buddhist concept of time. We call the world *sansar*. The word *sansar* means the wheel, that which comes back again and again. Every event returns in infinite repetition. It has been before, it will be again.

Only the unrepeatable, the unique, becomes historic. To Christians, Jesus is a historic personality. He cannot be repeated. But for Indians, Ram is not a historic personality. Ram will be repeated in every age. In the same way, *tirthankaras* are not historic for Jainas. They appear in every age; there will be a repetition, the same thing will go on and on and on. It has always been the same, so no event is particular and individual and worth recording. To record it makes no sense.

But there are jumps in this circular progression, there are people who jump out of history. These people are religious. A person who is part of history is a political being. Politics is always of time, it can never go beyond time. But religion is never part of time. It is always beyond.

A person who has moved into an inner evolution may appear in history, but the moment of his realization is a spiritual phenomenon. When it happens, he is beyond history. That is why no record has been maintained of when Krishna was born or when he died. It makes no sense to us to record it. Any date will do, the date itself is meaningless because the date is part of

CONSCIOUSNESS: LIVING IN A VERTICAL DIRECTION

history, of time, and the person himself is beyond time. In whatever way the record of the happening is maintained, howsoever accurate it may be, it is meaningless because it cannot record that which is worth recording. That is always lost. And what is the sense of recording dates, years, places, names?

In the West, because of the linear concept of time and because there is so much obsession with temporal events, they have maintained very accurate records. But now the gap is beginning to be felt. The record is accurate, but something is missing. We know when Christ was born and we know when he died, but we still do not know who Christ is, what this phenomenon of christhood is. The phenomenon itself escapes us. We know the moment; the phenomenon itself is beyond time.

A Buddha is never misunderstood like Jesus because we always know that no matter what he is talking about, he himself is something beyond time. We never misunderstand him, because we know this. But Jesus was very much misunderstood. When he said "the kingdom of God," people misunderstood this as being a kingdom of this earth. When he said, "I am the king," he was talking about a phenomenon beyond time, but people understood that he was proclaiming himself the king. Jesus was crucified because his non-temporal words could not be understood. People only knew events; they understood his words in terms of time.

In India, neither Krishna nor Buddha nor Mahavira were crucified, not because their teachings were less revolutionary than Jesus', but because we knew that they were not talking about *this* world. We understood that their words were meant for something that is not of this world. If they said, "I am the king," we knew what they meant.

If Krishna says, "I was, always. There was no time when I was not," we understand what he means by that. But when Jesus says, "I was, before Abraham," what he was could not be understood; it was impossible. There is a gap of a thousand years between Abraham and Jesus – how could Jesus have been before? In terms of time it is absurd, but in terms of existence it has a deep meaning. But the West could not understand it.

The Western attitude is still time-obsessed. There are reasons behind it. Why did time become linear in the West? – because the concept of rebirth never became prevalent. The concept was introduced so many times in the West. Pythagoras introduced it, but then it was lost; Jesus hinted about it, he talked indirectly about it – he never talked about it directly, he indicated it. But it could not be understood.

The concept of rebirth is the reason why the East could conceive of history in a circular dimension. If you are to be reborn again and again, there will be birth and death. Then birth will follow, and again there will be death. It will be a repetition. But if there is only life – birth followed by death, but death not followed by birth – then birth becomes absolute, death becomes absolute. Neither will come again. That is why time became so important in the West, and the West became time-obsessed.

These are all related things: history, time, tension. Why has the West become so tense about time? Not a single moment is to be lost, because once lost, you cannot find it again; it cannot be reclaimed.

The East is at ease: nothing is lost, everything can be reclaimed. You cannot lose it even if you try; things will come back. Death will be followed by birth again, you will be young again. Everything will come back, will return to itself.

This seems more natural. Every movement is circular – it may be of an atomic particle or it may be of a great star. Everything moves in a circle; there is no movement that is linear. Einstein talks of a limitless circular space. Even space is circular. Not only are things circular, but even nothingness – the vacuum itself – is circular, even the movement of a vacuum is circular. In fact, that which is not circular cannot move. Movement is circular.

The whole of nature moves in a circle. Summer follows again in the same course; each season comes and goes and is followed

CONSCIOUSNESS: LIVING IN A VERTICAL DIRECTION

in repetitive progress. Time cannot be different. Time is nothing but a medium of movement. If things are static, we will not feel time. We feel time, we become aware of it, only because things are moving. If we could be totally here for one hour, without any movement, we would not feel the passage of time. If you were always to remain the same age – if nothing moved, if everything remained static – then even eternity could not be felt.

You become aware of time because of movement. We cannot conceive of movement without time. Time means a sequence between moving events: something is followed by something else. This passage occurs in time. Since everything is moving in a circle, the passage of time cannot be noncircular.

History is an awareness of time: its events and their position in a particular framework – the framework of linear movement. People in the East became aware of linear time and of history only when the East came in contact with the West. Then the East felt that it was lacking something: "We have no history at all; we cannot create any history. Anyone can say that Buddha is mythological and we cannot prove that he is not. Anyone can say that Ram is just a story, a myth We cannot say that he is not because we have not maintained any record of when he lived. Where is the proof? We were not aware that any proof is needed." We became aware of it only when we came in contact with the West. We came to know that they have everything recorded, they have exact proofs. Only then, India began to write its history.

But still, a historic sense is not there. It cannot be, because with a circular time concept, history cannot exist. With an infinite opening toward the future, with an infinite possibility of repetition, a historic sense cannot exist. With the concept that death is just temporary – just a phase and not the end – history cannot exist. History can exist only with the concept of absolute death.

Then, each moment becomes significant. You have to live it otherwise it will be lost. Tension follows; you become tense.

THE ETERNAL QUEST

How to live each moment so that it may not be lost? How to live it so that it may be lived to its fullest extent? You cannot be relaxed.

The West can never be relaxed unless its time concept changes. Unless death is just a passage for rebirth, unless each moment is a repetition, an infinite repetition, you cannot be relaxed. How can you be relaxed when a moment is going, passing, and it will not come back? And the paradox is that the more obsessed you become with time, the more tense you become and the less you can live each moment.

The moment is lost in tension; you cannot live it. You can only live each moment if you are relaxed, if you are not aware of time, if you are not obsessed with it.

The more obsessed you are with time, the more you will write history and the less you will live it. History, as it exists – and it cannot exist otherwise – this history, this historic attitude, can never confront those phenomena that are beyond time. Even life is beyond time. It passes through time, but it is always beyond it. It is like a lotus leaf: always in water, but still beyond water, untouched by it. Life is like that. And the deeper life becomes, the more like a lotus leaf it is – always touching somewhere, but never touched; always in touch with time, but always beyond time. Untouched, virgin.

That is why we can have a record of political events but not of religious happenings. Religion can never have a history, only politics can have one. We can talk about Ghengis Khan, about Tamerlane; we can talk about Stalin, Mussolini, Churchill, Nehru. We can talk about them because these persons live in events, amidst events; they live in the world of form. But we cannot know any history, any real history, about a Buddha or a Jesus or a St. Francis. We cannot. And if you try to write about them, their lives will be uneventful compared to the lives of Ghengis Khan, Churchill, Stalin. Their lives will be eventless, totally vacant. Nothing happens.

Buddha sits under the *bodhi* tree. This is the event. But it is

CONSCIOUSNESS: LIVING IN A VERTICAL DIRECTION

nothing; the event is not worth writing about. If he is allowed to continue to sit under the *bodhi* tree, he will sit under it eternally. He will just be there – just sitting, not doing anything. Ages will come and pass, and he will still be sitting there just like a stone. That is why we have erected stone Buddhas and stone Mahaviras. It is not just an accident that Buddha is carved in stone. It is not accidental, it is meaningful. As far as Buddha's outward life is concerned, he was like a stone to us.

There is no difference between a stone Buddha and a real Buddha as far as the world of events is concerned. It makes no difference at all. On the contrary, you will be more attached to the stone Buddha because a living Buddha, sitting just like a stone, will be more troublesome. You will not be able to bear it, will not be able to tolerate it. You will think that a stone Buddha is better. You know that he is stone, so of course he is just sitting. No event is possible – that is why no event is happening.

A real Buddha is also a stone Buddha as far as time is concerned. He is just a face. All that is meaningful is beyond the grasp of history because he is beyond the grasp of time. There is an evolution – spiritual, religious.

There is a progression to political events, a mechanical accumulation. Civilizations come and go, forms change, but there is no evolution in it, there is no qualitative change in it. Nothing changes really, only the form changes. But because of the change in form, a fallacious myth of progress is created. It looks as if things are progressing. Nothing is progressing. Only forms go on changing.

You go on changing your clothes and create a façade that you are changing. The change of clothes is not a change in you. Even a change of education is not a change in you; even changing your house is not your change. Everything can change and you can remain the same. Then, spiritually, no evolution has occurred.

On the other hand, everything can remain the same outwardly and you can change. No one will know it, no one will become aware of it, because outwardly everything is the same, but the person is transformed, he has undergone a metamorphosis. He is a new person; the old one is dead. It is a resurrection.

We recognize change only when form changes. But we never recognize, we never become aware, if the spirit changes. And real progress is vertical, it is not horizontal. Form changes in horizontal lines, spirit changes in vertical lines. Form goes forward, spirit goes upward. The progression of history is just like a bullock cart: on and on, but on the same level. It is not vertical. It is not jumping from one level to another.

Two more things will also have to be understood. As far as form is concerned, as far as history is concerned, progress is collective, but as far as spirituality is concerned, progress is individual. You cannot evolve collectively. You can go forward, you can go backward, but you cannot go up collectively.

A spiritual happening is individual. That is why when someone takes the jump, when he becomes enlightened, he goes beyond our grasp. We have not jumped with him; there is no communication. He is somewhere that we are not so communication becomes impossible. He cannot communicate what has happened to him. He tries but fails, and feels the failure.

He uses our language, but with a very different meaning. We cannot grasp the meaning. We can understand the words all right, but because we cannot understand the meaning, the words become the basis of misunderstanding. He is using them with quite a different meaning.

For example, Christ talks about a kingdom. We understand what is meant by "a kingdom," the Roman governor, Pilate, knew very well what is meant by "a kingdom." He was an educated person, one of the most educated of those days. He knew everything; he was more educated then Jesus himself. Jesus was an uneducated man, a villager, a carpenter's son. Those who crucified him were cultured, educated, civilized, but they crucified him because they could not understand what he was talking about. They asked him, "Are you the king of the Jews?"

He said, "Yes. I am the king. Who else can be king?"

CONSCIOUSNESS: LIVING IN A VERTICAL DIRECTION

Of course he was, but in a very different sense. As far as the outward form is concerned he was a beggar and nothing more, but as far as the spirit is concerned he was a king. Those who thought themselves to be like kings were more like beggars. So he said, "Yes, I am. Who else can be?"

And whatsoever he was saying, he was saying with much consideration. He was right, a hundred percent right. But those who heard him just laughed. Either he was mad, or a very cunning fellow.

At the last moment, Pilate asked him, "What is truth?" Pilate was well versed in philosophy, he knew all the definitions – what is meant by truth – but he asked Jesus, "What is truth?"

It was right before Jesus went to the cross. Jesus just looked at him and didn't answer. He knew very well that whatever he answered would lead to more trouble, more misunderstanding. If he had been silent all along, it would have been better. Whatsoever he had said had come to be understood as something that he had never meant. And these people who were crucifying him were all educated, they were all well cultured. They were people who knew.

Pilate asked again, "Tell me, what is truth?"

Jesus remained silent.

This silence is very meaningful. He was not a silent person; he was always ready to answer. He never lost an opportunity to talk about the kingdom of God and the truth about God. But now he remained silent. It was a silent commentary, a silent verdict of a great failure. He had been saying things that were not understood. Each word he had uttered had led to a new misunderstanding.

Truth is individual. That is why it is incommunicable. And because it is individual and not collective, society is not interested in religion at all. It appears to be interested, but it is not interested. It shows interest to the extent that religion, too, can be made into a social affair. Otherwise society is very antireligious. Whenever there is an individual who is really religious, society goes against him. It begins with a sort of religious façade – a deception – but whenever there is a religious individual or a genuine religion, it goes against them.

It cannot tolerate a Christ but it tolerates popes, because popes are not religious at all. It can tolerate priests, but it cannot tolerate enlightened persons. Popes, priests – all the so-called organized religious sects – all create a deception, a false illusion of being religious. They create a sort of respectability.

Society is never interested in religion because religion is individual and society is always afraid of individuals. It is fearful of individuals, it is fearful of spiritual persons, because they go beyond society. They are rebellious, but not consciously, not knowingly. The very nature of a religious mind is rebelliousness. Religious people are not against anybody, they are not destroying things. They are not destructive in the least. Really, they are the only creative minds, but their very existence is rebellious.

Society will not allow genuine religiousness. It will only allow the false faces of religion. Society creates civilizations, not religion. Civilizations can have a history, but religion has no history at all. It only has certain religious individuals that exist here and there. Sometimes someone takes a jump, becomes a flame and goes beyond. But the moment someone, somewhere, becomes a flame – a spiritual flame – the moment he goes beyond our so-called world of forms, he becomes one with all the flames that have ever gone beyond. Jesus is a different person from Gautam Buddha, but Buddha is not a different person from Christ. They are one flame.

Another thing: religious evolution is not collective. It is individual, yet universal. That is what makes it look so mysterious. It is not collective, it is individual, but it is still universal because the person who undergoes the religious evolution is annihilated. He transcends collectivity but becomes one with the universe. He becomes cosmic, divine.

This divine phenomenon cannot be recorded. We have tried to record it, but all that we have succeeded in recording is just a

CONSCIOUSNESS: LIVING IN A VERTICAL DIRECTION

bare outline. It looks absolutely dead.

What do you know about Christ? – that he was born into a poor carpenter's family. Nothing else is known about him until seven years later, and then only one event is known: that he was missing during some festival and his mother and father were searching for him. Then again there is a gap and then, when he is thirty, some events are recorded. And when he is thirty-three, the crucifixion is recorded. This is all that is known about his life: his birth and one or two events, ordinary events of childhood, and then whatever he said after his thirtieth year, as recorded in the gospels.

Whatsoever he said... The moment something is uttered, it becomes part of time; it can be recorded. But where a person like Jesus is concerned, every record contradicts every other record. St. Luke says one thing, St. Mark says something quite different – because what is recorded is not exactly what Jesus said. Only what is heard by the recorder is recorded.

So there are some sayings of Jesus that are recorded and then there is the crucifixion. This is all of Jesus' life that is known. Compare this with it the life of Adolf Hitler. Then you will see what the recording of a life means: events, and more events, and still more events.

Is this record of the life of Jesus really a record? If this is really the record of the person Jesus was...it is such a bare, naked outline that no one seems to be behind it. It is not a biography, but only footnotes. The real biography is lost; only footnotes remain – something that is not substantial, something that can be complementary only if the substance exists. In itself, it is meaningless.

Jesus himself denied that anything that could be recorded about him was true. Once his mother and his brothers came to see him and someone said to him, "Your mother is asking to meet you, and your brothers have also come."

He said, "Who is my mother? Who is my brother? No one is my mother, no one is my brother."

THE ETERNAL QUEST

All that you can record is about the one who was born and yet Jesus said, "No one is my mother, no one is my brother, and unless you deny your mother, you will not be able to come to me."

Jesus said, "Unless you deny your mother, unless you cut yourself off from your father, you will not be able to come to me." He was saying unless you deny the life of the form, you can never know the life of the spirit. If you do not deny history, you cannot know the mystery of existence.

That is why history could not record what happened to Jesus. It cannot record such things. But history is not at fault. The phenomenon itself is such; it is completely transcendental to history. History goes on recording progress. This progress is a horizontal progress: the progress of things, the progress of scientific knowledge, the progress of medicine, the progress of health. All that is concerned with the outward form is recorded, but the inner cannot be recorded. And the inner is the real, the significant, the substantial.

The authentic spiritual evolution is with the inner. History is meaningless as far as spirituality is concerned. It is a political affair. By *political* I mean all that goes on outwardly. For example, the birth of Gautam Buddha is a political event, but his enlightenment is spiritual.

If you can see that the dimension of the spirit is a very different dimension, then you can understand that history is just a collection of events about the form, that it is just on the periphery, never at the center. Those cultures that have realized how shallow and limited history is have left it. They didn't bother to keep records. They said: "It is enough that Krishna was. It is enough. It is an eternal epic. And even if someone says that he was not, that he never existed, it makes no difference. If there is even a possibility that he ever existed, it is enough. If he can ever exist, even in the future, it is enough."

Jesus' life was recorded by those who were trying to record him historically. The record is very naked, fragmented, useless.

CONSCIOUSNESS: LIVING IN A VERTICAL DIRECTION

If you do not create a Christ of your own in your recording, then the record is meaningless.

Those who were writing about Krishna knew that the phenomenon was not historic, that they could not record it. But their record is very rich, it is very imaginative, it is very fulfilling. It is total in a way. How much they have written about Krishna! They could write it because there was no limit to it. There was no temporal limit, they were not bound by any temporal limits. They could be creative with it. No one could say what they should be writing. Something may never have happened, but they say that it need not have happened.

An epic was created around Ram, a story was created around Krishna. Everyone was at liberty. Valmiki wrote one thing; Tulsidas wrote something else. No one can say that they are contradictory.

Mark and Luke are contradictory because they are writing history. But Tulsidas and Valmiki are not contradictory. They are not writing history, they are not concerned with history at all. They are reliving – in their imaginations. They say, "We cannot say much. We cannot say enough because we are not capable. All that is said is only a fragment. It is not the whole story."

If you yourself see Krishna, you will see something else altogether. But you are at liberty to see it because the event is not historical. So the life of Krishna or of Ram becomes very rich.

Jesus' recorded life was very poor because his followers were obsessed with history. They could not write anything that was beyond history.

The Eastern mind could see that we cannot do justice to Krishna or Buddha if we limit ourselves to bare events. This will be an injustice because the real has happened somewhere else. Then how to record the real? It cannot be recorded, but we can create a myth, and that myth can indicate, can show something about it. Those who will read the myth will not read a bare statement of events. They will go deep into the poetry of the myth, deep into the imagination.

And it may be possible that somewhere – from their own imagination not from the facts, very far from the facts – from somewhere deep in their own unconscious minds, from what Jung calls "archetypes," they might get a glimpse, they may be able to know what has happened beyond history. They may be able to know, from deep down within themselves.

History cannot go deep inside you. Only poetry can. Only from within you can something happen which will be in sympathy with the non-temporal, which can be in communion with the non-historical. Krishna's life and Buddha's life are only jumping points to enable you to go deeply inside yourself.

If you read Tulsidas, a Western historian will say that this is not history, this is imagination. It is. But I still say that Tulsidas does more justice to Ram than Luke can ever do to Christ because he knows the secret. By going deeply into what Tulsidas has written you will again relive the whole phenomenon. Time will be transcended; you will again be in the time of Ram. Now there are no space/time relationships. Deep within yourself, you are in Ram's milieu – as if Ram was present, as if he was somewhere nearby.

That is why in India we perform the *Ram Leela* every year. We go on performing it every year just to create the same milieu again. When someone acts the part of Ram, it is not only that he is acting Ram. If you go into villages where the people have been untouched by today's concepts, the person who is playing Ram is Ram. The villagers behave with him as if he is Ram. They touch his feet. He is not an actor; he is Ram revived, the milieu is created. They will chant poetry, the whole story will be unfolded – the story that they believe in.

That, too, is miraculous. If you see a film two or three times, you will feel bored. And if it goes on again and again, you will go mad. But even though everyone already knows the whole story when the *Ram Leela* is unfolding, everyone is thrilled. If it were just a story or a drama, you would be bored. It is Ram – alive again, re-enacted. It is not only a stage but the whole

CONSCIOUSNESS: LIVING IN A VERTICAL DIRECTION

world. Ram has come again. It is as if you are living with him. The whole thing is being repeated. Everyone knows what is going to happen and, still, everyone is thrilled.

This is a rare phenomenon. It is almost impossible. Ordinarily you will not be thrilled about something that you already know is going to happen, but this is what happens in an Indian village. Villagers who see the *Ram Leela* are as thrilled as if something new is going to happen. It is not just a story. A certain milieu is being recreated and the villager who is seeing the play is not only seeing a drama. He is part and parcel of a great spiritual phenomenon. He is in it! The thing is unfolding and, by and by, his heart is unfolding

This is a mythological approach to the non-temporal: re-enacting it, reviving it, resurrecting it. History cannot do this, only myth can do this. Myth is helpful but not substantial. A creative imagination is needed to fill in the substance.

This attitude – the non-historical, mythological – is more in tune with the unconscious. History is in tune with the conscious, myth is in tune with the unconscious. Myth is in tune with the eternal, history is in tune with the temporal. History is yesterday's news and tomorrow's news. Today's news will become history: history is just an accumulation of news, a newspaper accumulation which goes on becoming greater. But history is unnecessary, spiritually unnecessary, because it can never grasp the significant phenomena. In another sense, it is not only insignificant but also dangerous, because the more you record the past as the past – and the more the accumulation grows – the more you are burdened, unnecessarily burdened.

For a moment, imagine that we could destroy the whole history of the world. Ninety-nine percent of our problems would disappear. They all come from the past. The Mohammedan problem, the Hindu problem, the Vietnamese problem, the Kashmiri problem, they all come from the past. It is sad but true that ordinarily ninety-nine percent of our lives are dictated to us through the grave. Those who have died are ordering the whole nonsense! If history were not given so much importance, much unburdening would happen.

Myth is needed. History is always of the past but myth is not only of the past; myth is also of the future. The form of the myth comes from the past, but the opening is always toward the future. If someone is thinking about Krishna in terms of myth, he is not only thinking about the past. He is thinking about the potentiality, about what is possible. Human consciousness can become krishna consciousness, it can evolve to that point. So myth is only nominally of the past. It always has an opening into the future.

History is always of the dead past. It has no future at all. But it dictates the future; the dead go on dictating. Stalin is still dictating, Hitler is still dictating. They go on dictating because of the obsession with history. If we can remove history they will not be able to dictate. We will be free of them, unburdened.

Myths should be continued, they open into the future. But history should be discarded: it should not be taught or thought about. It is concerned with absolutely unnecessary things, with nonsense. To me, all that is meaningful in the past must be made into a myth not a history. It must be thought about in terms of poetry not in terms of temporal events.

Poetry is never a closing. It is always an opening; it is never limiting. You can give poetry your own meaning. You have a certain freedom. But not with a newspaper: the more down-to-earth the record is, the less free you are. You cannot give it a meaning, you cannot relive it, you cannot create it, you cannot be creative with it. You can only be passive.

What can you do? Hitler is born in a particular year – how can you be creative about it? It is a dead weight; you can only be passive with it. But with Krishna, you can be creative. There is no date. In a way, he is never born. You can give birth to him at any time. With poetry you are at liberty, with myth you are at liberty. You can create, and when you create, you are also transformed. In creating, the creator is always transformed by

CONSCIOUSNESS: LIVING IN A VERTICAL DIRECTION

his own creation; he never remains untouched.

To me, history is a very worldly thing. Sometimes it is necessary, but usually it is an absolute burden.

Myth is a record of all that cannot be recorded, but that can be indicated. Some indications can be made. They have been made. Christianity would have been all the more rich if they had created a myth around Christ. But they could not create a myth. They were so obsessed with history that they could not add to it. They could not give a meaning to it; they could not develop or unfold the story. They were not even able to call it a story.

In India, we do not say "the history of Ram." We say "the story of Ram" – *Ram Katha*. It is not accidental. We give more importance to a story than to history because with a story there are possibilities. With history there is no possibility: it is a dead thing, it is already in the grave. A story is a living thing. You can do something with it, and it can also do something to you.

Because they could not create a myth around Jesus, Christianity could not really flower into a religion. Without a myth, no religion is possible. Christianity remained a clerical thing; it could not create *sannyasins*. It could not. It could only create preachers – trained, dead, disciplined, knowing. The beauty and the poetry of a *sannyasin* is not here, the original source is not there.

Because they could not create a myth around Christ, they tried to make a history out of him. Western history begins with Jesus; the very beginning of Western history is Jesus. That is why you calculate time "before Jesus" and "after Jesus." He is the midpoint, the calculation begins with him – after Christ, A.D.; before Christ, B.C.

The West tried to create history out of Jesus' life and they killed Jesus in the process. When they tried to deal with Jesus historically, it became absurd. They were not able to explain the miracles; the resurrection could not be explained. The attempt was bound to be a failure. They were not able to explain the miracles because miracles exist only in myths, they never exist in history. Because the Western mind was trying to create history, the miracles of Jesus became absurd, contradictory.

In India, if someone says that a dead person has returned to life it is not a miracle. It is an ordinary thing. After death, there is no way to move except to rebirth. Someone in India who reads about such a thing will definitely think in terms of rebirth. But in the West, Jesus became "resurrected," he came again to life. It became a problem that Christianity could not solve. They feel guilty. Something is wrong somewhere: how is it possible that a person who has died can come back to life? Because there was no myth surrounding it, the isolated phenomenon of "coming back to life" became absurd.

It is never claimed that Buddha was resurrected, nor Mahavira, nor Krishna – because everyone is going to be resurrected. It is not a miracle. If someone had said that Buddha is great because he came back to life, everyone would have laughed. Everyone comes back to life! This is not something to be talked about.

Fragments in Jesus' life appear to be contradictory. They cannot be explained. But if we call it *The Story of Jesus* rather than *The History of Jesus* there is no contradiction. Everything is possible in a story because logic is not needed. The only requirement is that the story be poetic, flowing. That is all; no logical reality is needed. The question of whether someone comes back to life again after crucifixion comes only if it is history. If it is a story, then there is no problem. Then, if someone says it is absurd, he himself becomes absurd. In a story you cannot raise questions. Only in a history can you raise questions and show contradictions.

Christianity would have been richer if, instead of history, there had been a myth surrounding Jesus. If there had been a myth, then Christianity would not have become such a political religion. It would have been more religious.

The source is there. You can go deep into Christianity and be revived by it. Then you will not only be a Christian by doctrine, you can become a Christian by unconscious communication.

One thing to be noted is that whenever someone in the West goes deeply within, goes deep into his unconscious roots, he becomes an Easterner. The very quality of the mind changes. Jesus is an Easterner, Francis is an Easterner, Eckhart is an Easterner, Bohme is an Easterner. It makes no difference where they are born, the quality of the mind changes. On the other hand, whenever an Easterner becomes superficial, his mind becomes Western. Events become very meaningful to him, things become very meaningful. All that is on the surface becomes significant and all that is deeper is denied, negated.

The person who lives at his depths can accept all that is on the surface, but the person who lives on the surface cannot accept all that is deeply within him, because the very acceptance will be humiliating. To acknowledge that he has deeper depths within him will be a proof that he is only living on the surface. He will deny it. But a person who lives at his depths can accept the surface. He can say, "Yes, it is true. It is there; it exists. But deeper layers are there also. It is not everything."

History is just on the surface because time is on the surface. Consciousness is at the very depths. Then there is no time. But this will be more meaningful to you when you go deep into meditation. Then you will feel that your time sense is lost. By and by, you will feel that time is stopping. Finally a moment comes when there is no feeling of time. Time has stopped! Somewhere on the surface it is still going on, but inside, it has stopped. Then you yourself will be able to understand clearly what is meant by "a spiritual evolution that transcends time."

When we live in time, in the world of events, if someone is not doing anything it seems as if *he* is not. Doing is everything. Doing is in the realm of history, but being is in the realm of the spirit. You are; you just are. You are not doing anything, not even mentally. Nothing either physical or mental is happening. There is no doing at all, no ripple of action at all; you are in an absolute non-doing state. But you *are*.

This "beingness" is the vertical dimension. Through this "beingness" you jump into the unknown, into the divine. And unless one jumps into this non-historical, non-temporal moment, one has not known what life is.

7

The Disease Called Seriousness

Osho,
Life is tremendously serious...

NO, LIFE IS NOT SERIOUS. You are serious. Life is very nonserious; nothing can be more nonserious than life. Life is absolutely nonserious!

Osho,
But certain things have been achieved only because a person has been – maybe the word serious is not good – but the person has been really intense.

Intensity is a very different thing from seriousness. If you are serious, you can never really be intense; you can only be tense. That's a different thing. With seriousness, you can never be intense and deep. With seriousness, you will always be shallow.

Life is not serious at all. Life is just a nonserious play – with nothing to be achieved, with nowhere to reach. It is just a play, with no end. Seriousness is always end-oriented. It means you are living in order to achieve something, and life will be meaningless if you don't achieve it.

This is seriousness: the meaning lying in the end, not just here and now. The end must be achieved. If you achieve it, then it is okay. If you don't achieve it, then everything is lost. So you are serious because you have made a point somewhere, and with

THE DISEASE CALLED SERIOUSNESS

it you have identified the whole meaning of your life.

You can never achieve anything, because nothing is static, everything is changing. You fix something today; tomorrow nothing is going to be the same, not even the planner. The whole will have changed completely; the end will remain only in your mind. The whole situation has changed now so you can never achieve it. That is why there is so much frustration

You try, you think, you plan, you work – and then there is no achievement. The very thing that you desire never comes into your hands. It can never come. If life were a static and fixed thing, not dynamic and flowing, then you could achieve it – but then life would be a death. Life is life because it is dynamic, changing. You cannot predict its course. I is unpredictable. That's what we mean when we say it is dynamic and flowing; it is always flowing into nowhere.

If you are serious, then you cannot flow. Then you are frozen inside; then you become just a dead stone. Then there are resistances around you. You cannot melt, you cannot be. As life changes, transforms, you cannot transform and change yourself with it. You have a fixed pattern, a fixed shape. Now the shape will be the resistance. Then there will be a struggle. Seriousness creates frozenness; frozenness creates a struggle. You cannot just let go.

So be ready to be any shape or form. Any shape or form is good: trees are good and dogs are good and man is good. Be ready to be in any shape or form, then you will be living more and living intensely – because intensity is killed when you become identified with a particular form. Then you are shallow because you are concerned with the form, not with the being. Then you will be tense, not intense.

It you are ready to be any shape whatsoever then there is no surface to you: there is no shape and no form. You are ready to be in any form. Then you begin to live inwardly and you can flow with everything. And the more you can flow, the more alive you are.

THE ETERNAL QUEST

So to me, life is not seriousness at all – but religious people have made it serious. That's why religious people are basically antilife. But to me, that is not religion, that is just a metaphysics for suicide – it is suicidal. To me, religion means a very nonserious attitude – very childlike in everything, very innocent.

A serious person can never be innocent, and one who is innocent can never be serious. They are contradictory; they cannot exist simultaneously. A child is never serious, but very intense, in everything intense. If he is playing he is intense; if he is angry he is intense, if he is loving he is intense. But an old man is never intense. He is serious. Even when he is playing he is serious. He will turn play into work because the play will become a fight, a struggle, competition, defeat and victory – everything will come, every nonsense will emerge. It will not be just a play.

So intensity is something else. It is not seriousness. With seriousness, sadness is always about to come. You cannot enjoy seriousness, you cannot be happy with seriousness, you cannot laugh with seriousness. That's why saints have never laughed. With seriousness, sadness is always bound to be somewhere around the corner.

Seriousness is sad, it cannot laugh. And even if it laughs, it is only a release mechanism and the laughter is not innocent – it is only a release mechanism. A serious person can laugh, but then it is only to release the tension of seriousness, and then again he is ready to be serious. Tensions are accumulated.

If I tell a joke, then I create tension in you, expectation, curiosity. What is going to happen? How will the thing turn out? So you become tense with expectation. You become serious, and your mind begins to work – what is the end going to be? And if the end turns out just as you have expected it to, you will not laugh because then there is no release. If the end turns out to be completely unimagined, if the end is just a turning, a complete turn; if you could never have expected that this will be the end, then the tension which has come to a climax is

THE DISEASE CALLED SERIOUSNESS

released. You laugh. That laughter is not innocent, because that laughter is just a by-product of tension. So every joke has to create a tension in you. Then you feel released.

But innocent laughter is something very different. It is not a release mechanism, it is just a way of living. It is just a way of living!

Take laughing as a way of living. Exist as laughter; you will be absolutely nonserious. It may be that you may not be able to achieve anything, but what is the meaning of achievement? Even one who achieves – what does he achieve? Even by achieving, nothing is achieved. Then the whole absurdity is this: even if you achieve something, nothing is achieved and much is lost.

The person with a non-achieving mind gains much without gaining. Every moment he is gaining. Whatsoever he gains will not be something very visible. In the end he may not have any achievement in his hand, any award, but he will be rich inside: every moment was rich living. The achievement is in the being, not in the playing. He may not be a great man, a very famous man, a great scientist, a great painter; he may be no one really, but he can die peacefully; he can die lovingly. He is rich inside. Life has given much, as it was. Nothing was snatched, nothing was taken with a struggle. As life was, it has given much. It was a blessing, it was a beatitude, it was a benediction as it was, without any conditions.

The mind that is trying to achieve is saying to the whole of life, to the whole cosmos, "I can be happy only if this is fulfilled." The person is living with a condition.

You cannot live with conditions toward the whole. You will never be heard. You will never feel any resonance from the whole if you have any conditions. Your own condition will become a stone around your neck. You will be crushed under it by your own hands. It is not that the whole crushes you; you crush yourself with your own stone. And you create a barrier: the whole cannot flow in you because you have a condition. You say, "Come in, but fulfill this much." The whole cannot flow in you, you cannot flow in the whole. Then everything is crippled and diseased.

So don't place any conditions on the whole; don't make any bargains with the whole. Don't be a competitor with the whole, don't struggle with the whole. Then you are holy. Flow into it and let it flow into you – unconditional movement, unmotivated movement, out and in, just like breathing. Then you will be nonserious, but intense. Then you will be living, but blissfully. Then there is no possibility of sadness. Then there is no seed of frustration. It is impossible. No one can frustrate you, and whatsoever happens is good. Then good is not against bad; then good is just a feeling – whatsoever happens is good. Then there is nothing against bad, against good.

This I call a religious mind – nonserious, playful, innocent, without any struggle. But the whole concept that we have is of a very serious man.

Someone wrote me a letter yesterday. He writes that he believed in someone as if he was *bhagwan*, a god, and he believed continuously for fifteen years. And then one day he saw that he was angry.

So he writes that on that day, not only did that man become just human – not a god – but from that day: "I cannot believe that any human being can ever be *bhagwan*, can ever be a god."

So I have written to him that there are two possibilities. "A person, you have believed as divine became angry, so there are two possibilities: either this man is not divine, or your definition of divine was wrong!"

But no, your definition can never be wrong: "This man is wrong!" Your definition is more solid than fifteen years of faith and trust.

Your definition…but who says that the divine cannot be angry? Who says? We don't know what the divine is, but we fix the definition. Who says that the divine cannot be angry? Of course a divine person must be angry in a divine way – that's another thing!

THE DISEASE CALLED SERIOUSNESS

But we have definitions. And life always transcends all definitions so we are frustrated.

So I have written to the man that that person was very honest: "He could be angry before you." It is very simple not to be angry in front of a person who has believed in you as *bhagwan* for fifteen years. It is very simple not to be angry. It is not such a difficult thing. But he was very sincere, he flowed, he could be angry.

Rinzai, a Zen master died. Then his disciple, the chief disciple, began to weep. So there were at least one *lakh* people there. They were very frustrated because this disciple was known to be a person who has realized, so how could he weep? "He must not weep, because if a realized person weeps then everything is lost. Then there is no difference."

So some friends came and requested him not to weep because his whole image would be destroyed. But the disciple said, "When have I promised you that I should not weep? And was it a condition, that you will believe me to be realized if I don't weep? When was this promise made? So do two things: either decide that I am not a realized person, or change your definition so that a realized person can weep – of course in a realized way!"

Really, a person who lives at one with life just flows. There is no resistance. Anything that comes, comes; anything that happens, happens. He has no resistance. He is not going to say to life that this must not happen. He has okayed the whole. He has said yes to everything.

In the name of conflict, condemnation, struggle we have created images of divine persons, realized persons, according to our definitions. So if Mahavira laughs, then his disciples will feel something has gone wrong: it is inconceivable because according to the disciples' definition – a dead definition... And definitions can never be living because anything living changes, and definitions cannot change. And if a definition changes, then it is not a definition at all. It is fixed, and life is never fixed.

So don't think in terms of categories. Just think about one thing: you must be flowing and letting anything happen. Accept it. If you are going to be a loser, be a loser. If you are going to be defeated, then be one who is defeated. And if you are ready to be defeated, to be a loser, then no one can defeat you, because then the whole thing becomes nonsense. Losing is meaningful because winning is meaningful – because you have a stake in it, because you have made the decision to win. Then losing becomes hard. You feel defeated, frustrated.

So to me, a divine existence means: just flow. If you win, that is good. If you lose, that's good.

8

God: The Creative Process, Not the Creator

Osho,
We know from many sources, such as the Bible, that God created man in his own image. If he has created everything, everything must be good. Then where does the idea of wickedness come from?

SO MANY THINGS WILL HAVE TO BE taken into account. Firstly, to think of God as the creator is to divide reality into two: the creator and the created. There is no division, no duality like this: the creator *is* the creation. The world and God are not two things: the creation is the creator. It is not like a painter. A painter creates a painting. The moment the painting is created, there are two things: the painter and the painting. Creation is more like a dancer: the dance and the dancer are one.

When you think about God in terms of duality, God becomes a false God. There is no God who is separate, apart, sitting somewhere, presiding, engineering, administrating beyond the world. The very world, the very being, is God.

The term *God* is anthropocentric; it is our creation. We have personified what is really a process. God is not a person but a process — constantly evolving, changing; constantly reaching beyond and beyond. God is a process. So to me God is the creative process, not the creator.

Human beings have thought of God in human terms. It is natural. We have said that God created man in his own image.

GOD: THE CREATIVE PROCESS, NOT THE CREATOR

If horses could think, they would deny this: they would say that God created horses in his own image. Because man has created the philosophy, he has made himself the center of it. Even God must be in our image; he must have created us in his own image. Man's ego has asserted these things; this is not knowledge, this is not knowing. This is simply an anthropocentric feeling.

Man feels himself to be the center. We think that the earth is the center of the universe and man is the center of creation. These conceptions are false imaginations, dreams of the human ego. God has not created anybody in his own image because the whole is his image. The trees, the earth, the stars, the animals, men, women…everything that exists is his image, not just man.

Then too, we have divided the world into good and evil. The world is not so divided. Good and evil are our evaluations. If man did not exist on the earth, there would be neither good nor bad. Things would exist, things would be there, but there would be no evaluation. The evaluation is man's. It is our imposition, it is our projection.

We say that something is *good* or something is *bad*. But as far as creation, the creative process, is concerned, everything simply *is*. There is no good, there is no bad. The night is not bad, the day is not good. The darkness simply is, the light simply is. These are not two things – distinct, apart and opposite – but rhythms of one thing. The darkness and the light are both waves of the same reality. For existence, darkness is not evil. But for us it is evil, because our fearful minds have always been afraid of darkness.

Nothing is bad. We say that life is good, and death is bad – but how can that be? Death is the pinnacle of life, death is the peak of life, death is part and parcel of life. There can be no living process without the dying process. Death and life are not two things, but two poles of a single, unitary process.

We are afraid to die so we say that death is evil: "If God has created the world then there must be life and no death." But if that had been possible, it would be the most boring existence. If there

THE ETERNAL QUEST

were only life and more life – and no death – then we would pray to God to give us death, because there is a moment to live and a moment to die; there is a moment to come up and there is a moment to go down. There is no peak without the abyss.

But we only want the peak and not the abyss. That is not possible. These are two aspects of one reality: the evil and the good. So do not impose your own feelings, your own evaluations, on the creative process. Rather, if you want to know the creator, the creative process, go beyond yourself, beyond these dualisms. Do not think in terms of duality. When you go deeply into something, when you go to its very depths, the evil changes into good and the good changes into evil. These are just two waves of the same reality, two different patterns of the same reality.

For example, if I become diseased, to me it is an evil. But to the germs that are the cause of my disease, it is life – and good. Who is to determine whether it is good or bad – me or the germs? If I become healthy the germs are bound to die, so for those germs my health is an evil and for me the life of the germs is an evil.

But to God, existence, the germs and I are the same. So there is no evil for him, no good for him. He lives in us, he dies in us. He is the darkness and he is the light. That is why he is the transcendental, the beyond. That is why he both is and is not.

Our minds always think in terms of dichotomies. They cannot think without dividing. Whenever we go to think about something, we dissect it, we divide it into two. That is the methodology of the mind. Mind cannot think in terms of unity, in terms of synthesis. Mind thinks in terms of analysis, so everything passing through the prism of the mind becomes divided.

Just like the light is one but through a prism it is divided into seven rays, so too the prism of the mind divides everything. That is why, if you want to know and realize that which is undivided, you have to go beyond mind.

Do not use your mind as the instrument. It cannot lead you beyond duality. If you use the mind, there will be a creator

GOD: THE CREATIVE PROCESS, NOT THE CREATOR

and that which has been created. This division is false and because of this false division you create false problems and false theologies. You create problems and then you think about the solutions. Because the problems are false, the solutions are bound to be false.

All theologies are based on dualistic concepts. That is false. Religion is not theology. A theology can be Christian, a theology can be Hindu, a theology can be Buddhist, but religion itself is the realization of the whole. It is not divided into Christianity, Hinduism or Buddhism.

Theology is based on a false assumption: an assumption of duality. Then, problems arise. First you divide existence, which creates problems. Then you go on solving the problems endlessly. But there is no solution. No theology has come to any conclusions; every theology has moved deeper and deeper into falsehoods.

That is why the new generation has come to a point of discarding all theologies: Christianity, Hinduism, Islam... The new generation have come to a breaking point where they want to discard all the falsehoods that theology has created. You have created the problems and you have created the solutions, but you have not asked the basic thing: whether the problem is authentic, or whether it has been created because of your mind; whether the problem is your creation or whether it is really a part of the reality.

In reality, there are no problems so there is no need for any answer. When you think, there are problems. When you do not think but you realize, there are no problems.

So religion is a process to go beyond thinking, to achieve a point in your mind where there is no thinking at all. You are, but without thoughts. You are in a state of mind that can be said to be a state of no-mind, a state of no mental processes.

A mind that is not thinking is a mind that is in meditation. That is the meaning of meditation. To meditate means to go beyond your thinking process. The moment you transcend the thinking process, you come to a realization; you come to feel that which is. Philosophy cannot exist without thinking, and religion cannot exist with thinking. Philosophy thinks, religion knows.

Thinking means a mind that does not know. A blind man can think about the light and go on thinking about it, but he cannot come to any conclusion because he cannot *really* think about it. You can only think about something you have known – but when you have known it, there is nothing to think about. That is the dilemma, the predicament; that is the basic puzzle. A person who knows never thinks, because there is no need to think. What you know, you know. There is no need to think about it. Only a person who does not know, who is ignorant, thinks. But how can you think about what you don't know?

A blind man goes on thinking about light, but he cannot really think about it. He cannot imagine it, he cannot dream about it, because he has not known it. Light is foreign to him. A blind man cannot even think about the darkness, because even to know darkness eyes are needed. Without eyes, you cannot know the darkness. A blind man knows neither the darkness nor the light.

Ordinarily we think that a blind man lives in darkness. No, there is no darkness for a blind man. Darkness is as much a perception of the eyes as the light. You cannot say to a blind man that light is opposite to darkness because that, too, will be unintelligible to him. A blind man can know light only by becoming able to see. Thinking cannot become seeing.

In reference to this, one thing must be said. In India we have called philosophy *darshan*. *Darshan* means seeing. We have not called philosophy thinking; we have called it seeing. In Europe the term *philosophy* carries another connotation. *Philosophy* means love of knowing, love of thinking. There is no parallel term in Western languages for *darshan*.

A new term has been coined by Herman Hesse. The term is appealing. The new term is *philosia*: the love of seeing. *Sia* means to see. *Philo* means love, and *sophy* means thinking. So

GOD: THE CREATIVE PROCESS, NOT THE CREATOR

philosophy means love of thinking. We have no term in India for it. We cannot translate the word *philosophy* into any Indian language. Our term is *darshan*. It means seeing, not thinking, but seeing.

Seeing comes not through the mind, but at the moment the mind is annihilated, the moment the mind is not, the moment the mind ceases. Every type of seeing – either of science or of philosophy or of religion – is an outcome of the state of no-mind.

We have known the example of Archimedes. He was thinking and thinking, and came to no conclusion. Then he was lying in his bathtub. Suddenly, something was seen. He ran out of his house naked. He had seen something, and he ran into the street crying, "Eureka, eureka! I've found it, I've found it! I've achieved!"

If you ask an Einstein or a Picasso or a Hesse, they too will say that something has been seen; whether in poetry or in painting or in scientific discovery, something is seen. And the moment of seeing is not the moment of brooding, the moment of seeing is not the moment of logical thinking. Logical thinking is held in abeyance. The logical mind is not working, and suddenly, something overpowers you, something comes to you – or you go somewhere, somewhere beyond the human limits. Then you know; knowing is there.

So do not create dichotomies. First you create dichotomies, then you create problems, then you go on solving them. And then of course, as a logical consequence, theologies are created and there are theologians, teachers, professors, gurus, and the whole nonsense, the whole nuisance. So to me, there is no problem. The problem itself is false.

Osho,
You said that God is the creative process. Then why are things created? What is the purpose of creation, or is it something that just exists?

THE ETERNAL QUEST

If God exists as a person then the question why becomes relevant. If God is a person then we can ask, "Why have you created the word?" But God is not a person; God is a process. You cannot ask the process, "Why do you exist?"

Existence exists without any cause. Thinking in terms of causes leads nowhere. If you go beyond one cause, then there is another cause. If you go beyond that, then another cause comes. And the why remains – always, endlessly. You ask why, and again you are confronted with another why.

If God is a person then the why becomes relevant. But God is not a person. You cannot ask him; you *are* him. You yourself are the cause.

Existence is uncaused; otherwise you will have to invent ultimate cause – but that carries no meaning. If you say that there is an ultimate cause, it means that beyond a certain point you will not ask again what the cause is. Even a person who believes in God as the creator, who says, "God created the world" may invent why's and answers. But if you ask him, "Why is there a God, why does he exist?" then the religious man will say, "God is uncaused. He is the cause, so he is uncaused."

Existence itself is uncaused. At the beginning there is no cause, so in the end there can be no purpose. Only when there is a cause can there be a purpose. There is no beginning – because if there is a beginning, then there must be a cause. Existence is beginningless. And there is no end because the beginningless cannot come to an end. It is endless. So there is neither a beginning nor an end to existence. It is eternal, uncaused, without any purpose.

For the human mind it is meaningless to say this, because we think in terms of causes, "from where?" and in terms of purposes, "to what end?" Because of this limitation of the human mind, it cannot conceive of something that is beginningless, endless, uncaused, purposeless.

But how can there be any cause, and how can there be any

purpose? To be is enough, to have been is enough, being is enough.

You can think of it in another way, through another outlook. When you love someone, you do not ask what is the cause of it. If love is caused by something, it ceases to be love. Love flowers uncaused. If a cause could be pointed out, then the beauty of love would be lost, then there would be a scientific explanation for it.

You cannot ask what love is for. There is no purpose in love. If I love you, I cannot ask why. If I am loving you for some reason then it is not love. Love is purposeless.

In love, we come closest to godliness. That is why Jesus said, "God is love." It is not that "God is loving" – no. That is not the meaning. "God is love": in love, we come closest to the creative process, closest to godliness. Love is the peak from which we come to know what religion is.

Love is religious. So a person who cannot love, cannot pray; a person who cannot love, cannot be religious. Only a loving mind can be religious, because only a loving mind can think in terms of no purpose, no cause. Love is enough. It does not ask anything beyond itself. It is a fulfillment in itself; it is the end in itself. A single moment of love is eternity itself.

When we ask *why*, *where*, *how*, we are not asking religious questions. If you ask *how*, the question becomes scientific. The question *how* is the basis of science: how are things happening? And if you ask *why*, the question becomes philosophical.

Religion has no question. For religion, there is no questioning. There is a quest, but no questioning. There is a quest to know *what* is – neither why nor how, but what is.

Of course, to solve the question *how* is easier. We can go on solving and solving and there will be no end to it. Every solution will again create a problem. The how will again be encountered, so science will go on progressing. You cannot conceive of a day when scientists will come out of their laboratories and say, "Now, science has been achieved!"

Philosophers will go on thinking and thinking *why* and there will be as many answers as there are thinkers. If everybody on earth begins to think about it, there will be millions and millions of answers. Everybody can say, "Because of this or that."

But religion does not ask. Religion is a quest, not a questioning. It is a quest after what is – not after the beginning, not after the end. It is a quest for neither the cause nor the purpose, but for that which is – this very moment, here and now. The *what* is the quest.

A scientific mind can go on searching without ever changing itself. A philosopher can go on inventing answers without changing an inch. But a religious man cannot even begin without changing. The moment he begins to ask, "What is?" there is a change, a transformation – because he himself is part and parcel of what is.

You are neither part and parcel of the *how* nor of the *why*. You were not asked anything in the beginning, nor have you been asked to plan for the end. You are somewhere in the middle – in the "is." You are only concerned with what is, here and now, this very moment.

So religion is concerned with the present – neither with the past nor with the future. And the present is the only existence; the present is the only time. The past is memory; the future is imagination. The present is the only reality, the only existence.

Religion is concerned with the existential, the purposeless, the meaningless, the uncaused. Things are – and you can become one with them and can achieve a moment of bliss, a moment of pure existence, a moment of total consciousness. In India we have called this *satchitananda* – the moment of total existence, the moment of total consciousness, the moment of total bliss.

Once you have a glimpse of it, there will be no question, no problem. You will be at ease with reality. Then you will be in a state of let-go with reality. You will flow with it, you will live with it. You will breathe it, you will be one with it. You will be it.

GOD: THE CREATIVE PROCESS, NOT THE CREATOR

Osho,
What is death, and what exists after death?

If you think about what is, you will pervert it. If you think about it, then you will impose your own conceptions on it.

"What is" can be revealed only when there is no conception, no thought, no theory in you; when your mind is totally vacant; when your mind has become an emptiness, a nothingness; when your mind is just a womb, a receiver. When nothing from your mind is imposed, when your mind is naked and empty, only then is "what is" revealed, because there is no one to pervert it – no one to imagine anything, no one to dream anything, no one to project anything.

One must approach reality completely vacant and empty, without any preconceived thoughts, without any prejudices, without any preconceptions of what is to be there. You must go into nowhere; you have to go into nothingness. Only then does your mind become just a receiver, a receptivity. And then, what is, is revealed.

Even after that, when you have to assert it, express it, you will not be able to. You won't be able to express what has been known. Language is not adequate, words are not enough. Something so vast, something so multidimensional, something so unimagined, something so unknown, has come over you that you can be struck dumb. The greater the realization, the less the possibility of expressing it.

The truth has never been said. It has been known, it has been lived, but never said. No word, no scripture, has expressed it. They have tried, endeavored, taken pains to express it, but it has remained unexpressed, unknown. You can come to it only when you do not come with your scriptures; you can come to it only when you do not come with your theologies; you can come to it only when you do not come with your questions. A mute quest is required not a verbal questioning.

And you can come to it at any moment. When you are under

a tree – just sleeping, relaxing, doing nothing – you can come to it. Near a seashore – just sitting, doing nothing – and it can overwhelm you. Under the starry sky – just existing, just being, just present, not doing anything – it can penetrate you.

That is why there are glimpses of it in love. When you are in love, words cease, thinking ceases. When you are in love, something becomes silent in you. Then there is no communication, and still there is a communication. You are silent, but communicating. In your silence, something comes to you and something goes out of you.

Religion points toward total silence. One must be silent to hear the creative process: one must be totally silent to know that which is. Every moment we are thinking and thinking. This thinking creates a barrier.

If you are listening to me and still thinking within yourself, then there will be no communication. When I am answering you, if you are still creating new questions – comparing what I am saying, thinking about whether it is right or not – then we are poles apart, then there is no communication. Your thinking has come between us as a barrier, and that barrier cannot be crossed.

If you are just listening – and that is the miracle, to be just listening – then even this communication that is happening right now between us can become a communication of what is. If you are just here – present, doing nothing – then something from my eyes, from my hands, from the friends who have gathered here, from the whole situation that exists right here, can become an awakening, and you can come into contact with what is.

And you ask, "What is death?" One cannot know before dying. How can one know? You can think about it, but that will not be death, that will not be real. One has to die to know death, and one has to live to know life.

Do not think about death. While life is, live! Know life. And if you know it, then you will know death also, because death is

GOD: THE CREATIVE PROCESS, NOT THE CREATOR

the pinnacle, the peak of life, the completion of life. So do not ask what death is. It will come, and you will go through it.

But it is possible to go through death and still not know it. We are passing through life and still we have not known it. We are asking, "What is death?" while we are alive. The reverse can also happen: when we are dying we may be asking, "What was life?" A dying person asks what life was, and a living person asks "What is death?"!

A living person can come to know life. Know it, be one with it, absorb it, drink it completely, eat it! Then death comes. When you have known the day, the night comes. When you have known the day's awakening, you will have to know the night's relaxation and sleep. It is there, it is coming, it is hiding somewhere. It will come, but do not ask about it. Know what is here and now. Become a knower, a seer, so that when death comes, you will know it also.

A person who knows life, ultimately knows death also. And when he knows both, he knows that life is not against death nor is death against life. When he knows both, he knows that something unknown has come into being, and that something unknown has left. Birth has been a door and death, too, has been a door. Something – existence – has come in, and something has gone out. Nothing begins, nothing ends. There are births beyond birth, and there will be deaths beyond death. There will be births beyond death, and there will be deaths beyond birth. The process is endless, the voyage is eternal.

Know what is; do not ask what will be. How can you know it? – you can only think about it and create theories. Theories are unimportant, meaningless; feelings are potent, meaningful. So while you are alive, feel life. Then you will become capable of feeling death when you die.

It is as blissful to know death as to know life. It is as blissful to awaken in the morning as it is to go into deep sleep at night. Both are blissful. But you must know them while they are happening; you cannot know them beforehand. And if you ask someone, then what you know is secondhand – not a firsthand knowledge, not a felt knowledge, not a realized knowledge, not a knowledge that has penetrated your ultimate being, that has come to you through your innermost core. The real knowledge always comes through seeing, through knowing firsthand.

First know life; do not ask what death is. Know life, and by knowing life you will come to know death also. What you are transcends both. You are neither life nor death. You have been living, you will be dying. Your being transcends both.

Do not identify yourself with life. If you identify yourself with life then you will think of death as your enemy. Know life and then you know that you are beyond, unidentified – someone who has come to life. And you will know death, too, as a door going back, returning to the source.

Life comes, death comes, but the source remains beyond both.

> Osho,
> Can you tell us something more about the concept of God in Indian philosophy?
> What is truth?

As I have said, to me there is no such thing as Indian philosophy. And God cannot be represented by any idea; God is something beyond ideas. Every type of representation is a falsehood, a falsification. Every type of symbol is a dead symbol whether it is Indian or Western, Christian or Hindu. These are theologies not religion. Theologies are nothing but man's mental creations.

Pilate asked the same question that you have asked when Christ was going to the cross. He asked, "What is truth?"

A Christian will have an answer to the question, a Hindu will have an answer, a Buddhist, a Sikh…everybody will have an answer. But Christ remained silent, he had no answer. He remained silent; he did not answer the question "What is truth?" because the moment you answer it, it becomes a falsehood. It cannot be asserted. It can be known inside, it can be lived, but it cannot be asserted. Words, languages, expressions, are so feeble and dead that the living truth cannot be communicated through them.

Christ remained silent. But his eyes were not silent, his heart was not silent, his whole being was not silent. His whole being was expressing the answer, but Pilate could not see it. He knew only what was happening in terms of verbal communication. He would have known the answer to the question only if Christ had answered him through theology, through some theory – some image, symbol, concept. Pilate turned away. Christ remained unknown to him.

What I am saying is this: that every type of symbology, myth, every type of theological system, is the creation of the cunning mind, of the mind which calculates, systematizes, makes wholeness out of theories. But it is dead. This is not religion; religion is something alive.

Somewhere Nietzsche has said that Christ was the first and last Christian. He was the last Christian because nowadays a Christian is simply a Christian through believing in a particular dogma. A Christian is a Christian through accepting a theology, not through knowing the truth. Hindus, Buddhists, Christians, Mohammedans – they are all under the weight of tradition, of words, of verbalizations and languages. But to me, religion has nothing to do with words, language, scriptures. Nor is religion confined to any geography nor confined to any particular race. Religion is not confined to any savior, god, *avatar* or guru. Religion is available to everyone who asks for it, who is thirsty for it.

Everywhere – in every age, in every time, in every race, in every part of the world – religion is as available as the air, as available as the existence. One only has to be one with the existence to know religion.

THE ETERNAL QUEST

Osho,
What you have talked about seems quite modern.

What I am saying is not modern. What I am saying is as much ancient as it is modern. What I am saying is the eternal truth. It has always been said, it has always been felt. Buddha felt the same, Christ felt the same, Krishna felt the same.

But language becomes old, assertions become old. The Gita has become old, the Bible has become old, Buddhist scriptures have become old. Every age has to coin new words, new expressions. The truth remains the same; religion is eternal. It is neither old nor new.

What I am saying is not modern. Only the way of expressing it is modern. All expressions become old. The modern, too, will become old. It has already become so. The moment we have talked about it, it has become part of the past; it has become old. The new always has to be invented. It is necessary because every age requires a new language to be understood, every age requires a new terminology to communicate its experiences.

But truth is timeless. It is neither old nor modern, and it is as much Hindu as it is Christian; it is as much Moslem as it is Buddhist. To me, Buddha, Mohammed, Christ, when they come to know, know the same truth. But when they express it, their languages differ. That is natural. Buddha expresses in an Indian way, Christ expresses in Hebrew, Mohammed expresses in the Arabian way. Only the language differs, but because of the difference in languages, sects are created.

Then there comes to be an Indian religion and a non-Indian religion. There are at least three hundred religions on earth and three hundred languages. It is so. But three hundred religions? – that's nonsense! Religion can only be one, because nothing can be contradictory or opposite to the feeling of truth.

When I come to know it, I know the same truth. When you come to now, you will also know the same truth. But I will express it differently, you will express it differently. The

GOD: THE CREATIVE PROCESS, NOT THE CREATOR

difference is always in the expression, not in the experience. The experience is eternal. It is neither Hindu nor Christian.

These labels have become barriers to the universal, the one, the eternal, the endless, the beginningless. These expressions have become barriers. So every age has to discard the old prophets, the old traditions; every age has to invent its own ground to stand upon, its own heart to feel, its own mind to know and experience.

Expressions differ. The expression might be modern, but the expressed, or the unexpressed, is still ancient. What I am saying is ancient, not old; eternal, not old – because truth can never become old. It is always the living, the new, the young. It is always life itself.

9

The Need for Authenticity

Osho,
Is reincarnation a part of your teachings?

I DON'T TALK MUCH ABOUT DOCTRINES. I am not very interested in intellectual gymnastics. Reincarnation is a fact, but I don't talk much about it. I may help you to remember your past lives, but I don't make a doctrine out of it. If you can remember them then it is okay. If you don't remember them, that too is okay. But I don't talk about it. It is useless.

Osho,
You have said that belief is impossible today. Perhaps we can no longer believe in the same things that we believed in the past, but it seems to me that it is impossible to totally disregard belief. For example, don't you believe that what you are saying is true?

It is true, but I don't believe it. I know it. That's different. Knowledge is not belief.

Belief comes out of ignorance. You don't believe in the sun, but you believe in God. We do not need to believe that we are sitting here; we know it as a fact. But if I say that some ghost is also present, if you cannot see the ghost, you will either have to believe what I say or disbelieve it.

Belief comes only when you don't know. When you know, there is no question of belief. What I am saying is not a question

THE NEED FOR AUTHENTICITY

of belief. I know it is so; it is a fact. I don't insist that you should also believe it as a fact. I only say that you should experiment with it so that you can also come to know it as a fact.

Belief is basically concerned with ignorance. With knowledge, there is no belief. You do not "believe" in science. What would be the use of it? You don't "believe" that two plus two make four. Only fictions have to be believed, not facts.

What I am saying is a fact to me, but if I insist that you also believe it to be a fact because I am saying it... That kind of belief has become impossible, and it is good that it has become impossible.

> Osho,
> To me, if something is a fact then it is a fact for everyone. If it isn't, then it's not a fact; it's somebody's belief.

No, no. there are two types of facts: objective and subjective. For example, if I say that I love you, there can be no objective proof. How can I prove it objectively? Can any kind of detection prove that in my heart there is love? If I try to act in a loving way so that you will know that I love you, then I am just acting. How can it be proved objectively that I have love in my heart? But it still is a fact, a subjective fact.

Belief in someone else's subjective fact has become impossible. A Saint Francis or a Buddha may say, "I have achieved such and such," but he cannot show you what he has achieved. You can believe it or disbelieve it. Or, you can experiment and achieve the same thing – then you can believe it.

There is no objectivity possible as far as inner truth is concerned, so don't insist on it. That is what I mean. If I insist that my fact must be your fact, then I am a violent man. And if I say, "Believe it, because I know it is so", that is violence. I simply say what is a fact for me. I can tell you the technique of how it became a fact for me, how I came to realize it. I can tell you the technique. You can try it. If you also come to the same bliss, then it will become a fact for you.

Science is concerned with the objectivity of the fact. Religion is concerned with the subjectivity. A subjective experience cannot be shown. I cannot show you what I have attained; there is no way. Still, it is a fact for me, not a belief.

Osho,
Are values facts, or are they subjective?

Values must be based on your inner illumination. For example, Buddha says that to speak the truth is a value. For him it is an inner realization; it is not a question of faith.

He is not saying that if you speak the truth you will attain to heaven, he is not saying that if you speak the truth, God will be pleased with you. He is not giving you any profit motive. He is simply saying that when he speaks the truth he feels good, a well-being comes to him, and when he speaks an untruth he feels degraded inside, he feels suffering, he feels a bondage. This is his fact, subjective. And he says, "Try it. If you also feel the same thing, then it has become a realization to you." But just to believe in it because Buddha has said it is worthless.

This is my insistence, that unless something becomes a realization for you, it is bogus, and for you it is false. Don't follow phantoms. It is better to experiment and come to an inner truth than to go on following things that someone else has said. Don't be traditional. Be individual.

Religion is individual truth. You can be a Christian, you can be a Hindu, a Mohammedan, simply by belief. But that is bogus; you are not authentic. Simply by being born into a Christian family or a Hindu family you can be a Christian or a Hindu, but whatsoever you believe is borrowed. It is not authentic; you are not true to it.

THE NEED FOR AUTHENTICITY

So it is better to find out some small fact upon which you can be authentically based and you can say, "This is my knowing." That will transform your whole being. You may believe in many, many things, but they are not coming from your experience. Then you remain a false entity, a pseudo man.

When I say, "Make it your experience" I mean be authentic about it. A single fact that you yourself have realized will be transforming. You will be a different man; your feet will be on solid ground. That's why I don't insist on doctrines but on techniques. Doctrines are others' realizations. They may not be true. Techniques are simple methods; you can simply do them. If the technique works, if it is right, then you will come to the same conclusion.

Buddha was one of the most authentic men who has ever lived. His dying words were, "Don't believe in me."

Don't believe something because Buddha has said it, don't believe because others believe it. Unless it becomes a truth for you, don't believe it. That doesn't mean to disbelieve it. There is no need. Remain suspended. That is intellectual honesty: to remain suspended, to remain agnostic. Don't say yes or no until you come to know.

Believers are false, pseudo, inauthentic. That's why I say that faith has become impossible. To be authentic is to be religious – even if you have to say, "I don't know God, I don't know Christ, I don't know the Holy Ghost, I don't know anything. And because I don't know, I cannot believe. Unless I know, I will not believe."

Only this kind of attitude will create a situation for you to grow.

Osho,
You say that you have no beliefs. Yet you have a certainty that goes far beyond the probability that the confirmation of a hypothesis would allow you to claim.

THE ETERNAL QUEST

A hypothesis is not a belief. You need not believe in it; it is just a temporary thing. It may be true, it may not be true. There is no need to believe in it, the experiment will show whether it is true or not. You play with the hypothesis without belief, without disbelief.

As far as objective facts are concerned, an experiment can only lead to a certain probability. You can never know any objective fact in its totality. Something else may be discovered which can change the whole thing. So with scientific facts, your knowing always remains relative. You cannot be absolutely certain because the fact, any fact, is just a part of the great world, the infinite. In that infinity, whatsoever you know is always probable; it is never certain.

Science can never be certain. It will always be probable, because something new can always be discovered. You may destroy the whole hypothesis or change it. So science will remain probable. That is the very nature of it.

But religion can be certain because inner truths are not fragments. They are absolute in a sense: once you know them, you can be certain about them. There is no need to be certain, but you are certain. That feeling comes. It is just like when you fall in love. You never say, "I am probably in love." When you are angry, you never say that you are probably feeling, anger. When anger happens to you, you are certain of it; when love happens to you, you are certain of it. If you say that you are probably in love, then you are not in love. With love, the certainty comes automatically. The more you move inside, the more certain you become. The more you move to the outer, the more probable.

The further a thing is from you, the more probable it will be, and the nearer to you, the more certain. When you come to the very center, it is absolutely certain. That's why Jesus or Mohammed or Buddha is so certain; they are absolutely certain. And Einstein or any other scientist is absolutely uncertain. It is bound to be so. It is the very nature of the thing. The further removed something is from you, the less certain you will be about it.

THE NEED FOR AUTHENTICITY

When something happens to you at the very center of your being, there is no possibility of any uncertainty. You are absolutely certain that it is so. There is not even any need to be so certain – but you are.

Certainty is inner truth; probability is outer truth. Science will never be certain and religion will always be certain. That's why religion appears to be very dogmatic. It is bound to be. But don't try to enforce your certainty on others. That is irreligious.

An inner truth need not be believed, it only needs to be discovered. It is there already – you are it. And your inner truth is the only thing that can be truly known. Everything else will always remain probable.

If you allow me to say it, I will say that science is belief because it is always probable, and religion is knowledge because it is always certain. The only thing you can be certain about is your own self. If you cannot be certain even about yourself, you cannot be certain about anything else. If I am not certain that I am sitting here in this chair, then how can I be certain that you are here? You are removed from me; you may be just a dream. If I am uncertain that I myself am here, then I cannot be certain about you. All certainty starts with me: I am here. It is possible that I may be dreaming that I am here and I am not really here, but even to dream I have to be. That one thing is certain. You may be a dream, but I cannot be a dream because a dreamer is needed. The further you are removed from me, the more uncertain you will be. I cannot be certain about you; I can only be certain about myself. That is the only thing – what Descartes calls "the indivisible truth."

Science is belief. Religion is knowledge.

> *Osho,*
> *Jesus had a certain knowledge and Buddha had a certain knowledge. Yet their knowledge seems to be contradictory.*

Whatever Buddha or Jesus have said is not what they mean. To know the inner is one thing, but to put it into words changes it completely. Jesus uses a different language from Buddha; it is bound to be so. Buddha uses a different language because he is living in a different culture, a different world. But whatsoever they know is the same. You can compare Buddha's words with Jesus'. They are different; the language is absolutely different. Jesus uses Jewish symbolism, Buddha uses Hindu symbolism. They are different.

But if you have the same experience, then you can look beyond symbols and see that the experiences of Buddha and Jesus are the same. If you don't have that inner experience, then the languages will look different, contradictory.

A Christian scholar and a Buddhist scholar will never agree that the experiences of Jesus and Buddha are the same. But the problem is semantic, one of language. Eckhart will agree that the inner experience of the two is the same, Jakob Bohme will agree – because they themselves have achieved the same thing. Because they have achieved it, they can see beyond language. Language communicates, but it also becomes a barrier.

10

Life:
Unchartered and
Unknown Possibilities

Osho,
How can we become one with the reality and why are we separate from what is?

THE DIVISION IS SOMETHING that we ourselves have created. Reality has always been one; it has never known any division. All division is a mental division, a creation of our own conditioning. Reality has always been undivided, indivisible. It is still so. It has always been so, it will always be so. But through our cultivated minds, we feel it to be divided.

The moment you become whole, the moment you become aware, there is neither the individual nor the cosmic – or you can say that everything is the cosmic. The cosmic does not exist in opposition to the individual. Rather, all individuals dissolve in the cosmic.

Osho,
How can the cosmic be achieved?

By becoming aware of your fragmented mind, of your conceptions, your attitudes, your prejudices; by becoming aware of the mind that feels, hears, chooses. When you see a flower, it is not only that the flower is there. Between you and the flower, a particular mind exists, a particular attitude about the flower exists. Otherwise there would be no barrier between you and the flower. You would be one.

You and the flower are two extremes of one existence, two ends of one single moment. If your mind is not there, your consciousness and the flowering of the flower are two extreme points of one process. But if your mind is there – as it is always there – you are not just seeing the flower. Your seeing has a projection behind it, you are seeing in terms of your own conceptions, your own likes and dislikes.

You say, "This is a rose." But there is no such thing as "rose." The rose itself doesn't know that it is a rose. We are the ones who have called it that. And the moment you say "rose" everything that is associated with the word rose stands between you and the particular flower in front of you. The word has so many associations. If your culture says that a rose is beautiful, then the flower becomes beautiful. If your culture is against roses, then it becomes ugly. If your experience with roses is associated with pain from the thorns, then the rose becomes one thing. If your associations are happy, then the rose becomes something different. But all the while, the rose itself remains the same. You see it with your mind. Your mind destroys that which is real and creates something imaginary, hallucinatory.

If you have no mind, if you can see the rose without your mind, if your seeing is totally innocent, completely fresh; if your seeing is not coming from the past, if you and the rose are living simultaneously in this moment – if you are without mind: just aware, just existential – then the rose is not known as something separate. Then you know it to be part and parcel of your consciousness. Then the flowering of the rose is your own flowering; then the perfume of the rose is your own perfume, then your consciousness is the rose's consciousness.

The rose knows itself through you. Identification is not an act of dualism, but of total being. Through your consciousness, the rose has come to know itself.

This is the feeling. It cannot be expressed exactly, but the feeling is like this: that either you have flowered in the rose or the rose has become conscious of itself through you.

> Osho,
> Is this what is known as "seeing"?

It is really seeing. It is *darshan*, without the mind.

> Osho,
> That's the kind of thing Krishnamurti is always saying.

I don't know what he says, but I say: this is seeing. Only when you are mindless is seeing there. The mind is the destroyer, it is a destructive force.

So do not try to be whole. You cannot try. There cannot be any effort because every type of effort is the effort of one particular mind against other minds. That is why effortlessness has to be clearly understood. You cannot achieve it, because every type of achievement is the longing of a particular type of mind. You can only understand it. "This is so. This is the suchness."

The mind is fragmented. The mind is not one; it is polypsychic. You don't have a mind; you have many minds. These minds are the experiences of the past to which you have become attached, associated, to which you are clinging.

Why are you clinging? – because to exist mindlessly is dangerous, to exist mindlessly is insecure, to exist mindlessly is to always be in the unknown. That is why we have made everything that has become known to us a part of our consciousness. We cling to our experiences, our knowledge, so that we don't have to move into the unknown, so that we don't have to feel insecure about what is going to happen. We are clinging to that which has already happened. These are our safety measures.

The mind that is longing for security cannot be mindless.

LIFE: UNCHARTERED AND UNKNOWN POSSIBILITIES

This has to be understood. The mind that is longing for security can never be mindless because it will cling to past experiences, past knowledge, past information. You will always be living through a dead mind.

So there are three things to be understood. The first is that we do not have a single mind; we have many minds. Secondly, these minds are our past experiences. And thirdly, we cling to these multi-minds because of our fear of the unknown, because of the infinite possibilities of the future. The past is fixed because it has already happened. It is dead; you can deal with it. But you cannot deal with the future. The future is always unknown, uncharted. There are unknown, infinite possibilities about which you can never be certain.

Life means uncertainty, life means insecurity, life means to be in danger. Only a dead person is out of danger. Now he cannot become diseased, he cannot die, there is no death for him, he is at ease, everything has become certain. Now nothing else can happen, so there is no danger.

If you understand these two things – the certainty of the past and the uncertainty of the future – if you understand that life means uncertainty, life means insecurity, life means danger, life means uncharted and unknown possibilities; if you understand this, then by and by your minds will drop, they will cease to function, and you will become one, whole. By and by, your response will become total.

This total response is religiousness. It is a total response: every moment, in every situation. Be total within and be total without. The moment this happens, the totality within and the totality without become one. Then there is no barrier between you and the whole.

There can never be two perfections. The moment two perfections come close they become one. Wholeness is always one.

There is a saying in the Upanishads: "If you take the whole out of the whole, the whole remains behind." Nothing is taken out, because you cannot take anything from the whole. Even if you take the whole, the whole remains behind. And you cannot add anything to the whole. If you add something to the whole, it will remain the same.

There is no method to become one with the whole. You are already that. All methods are to help you to understand. They are to create a situation in which you can understand yourself: your multiplicity, your polypsychicness. When you know yourself in your totality, only then can you know what is beyond this totality.

So the first thing to be seen is yourself. It you have not even seen yourself, then seeing the wholeness is not possible.

> Osho,
> Will I be able to see the wholeness after doing meditation?

Yes. it will descend on you sometimes. When you are whole, the whole will explode in you. And this will go on becoming more natural as you continue to meditate. The gaps will be less, the intervals will be less. Finally a moment of explosion will come from which there is no escape.

> Osho,
> Can this happen through willpower?

Will is power, energy. There is no such thing as willpower. Will is power, will is energy. But by *will* I mean the whole. Those who use the term *willpower* use it in a psychic sense. They use it to mean the power of concentration. I am not using the term in that sense. To me, *will* means the whole.

So only the whole is will. We are never will; we are just desires. Will *is* power, without desire. It is power with no movement or power with an inner movement. It is power without

LIFE: UNCHARTERED AND UNKNOWN POSSIBILITIES

direction: directionless, dimensionless.

When we say, "God is power," it does not mean that God is powerful. It means godpower – "God" is the energy of the whole, the power of the whole. So when I say *willpower*, it does not mean that will has power. Will is power; it is energy. You can only attain it when you have lost yourself.

While you are there, desire will be there. Your power will come from your desires. It will be created by concentration, by narrowing, by exclusion. Then you will have moments of powerlessness also. Your potency will exist in opposition to impotency, so it will come and go.

But when will comes, nothing goes. Everything is. Even passivity is powerful, even impotence becomes potency. That is why the word *tao* is better then the word will and better than the word *dharma*. Tao is both death and life, both darkness and light, both potency and impotency. Only then does power become absolute.

Willpower, as it is ordinarily used, only means that power that is created by conflict, created by concentration. This is not power. It is just creating a conflict within you, and making one part of your mind in control of the other parts. A subtle energy, a subtle force, is created. You can use it, but then moments of depression, of powerlessness, will follow.

When there is no direction that you have to move toward, when you have no desires, you are power, you are energy, you are life. Then you exist without any shadows, without being followed by the opposite. That is why it is said that the whole is shadowless. It is, but there is nothing opposite to it that casts a shadow on it.

11

Hare Krishna, Hare Rama!

Osho,

Allow me to introduce us: Chidananda, Das Brahmachari, Das Adhikari, Indraram Das Brahmachari, Das Brahmachari. We are disciples of His Divine Grace. A.C. Bhaktivedanta Swami Prabhupada. All of us were born within the borders of United States and we became his disciples there in the last two to four years, we were initiated by him. Shri Agrawal extended an invitation to us to come here. We are not in knowledge what you might wish to do, so we are leaving the meeting up to you, and whatever you propose we will do it. Hare Krishna!

GREAT! HE WAS SAYING that you would like to ask something, so if you have any questions…

I can pose one question. I would like to know, can you describe to me what is your conception of the absolute truth?

No conception is possible about the absolute truth because every conception is bound to be relative. So the absolute transcends every conceptualization; you cannot conceive it. You can live it, you can be in it, but no intellectual conception is possible about the absolute. And any conception is bound to be erroneous because conception, as such, is relative. So I cannot say what my conception about the absolute is. I can only say no conception is possible about the absolute. The moment you go beyond conceptions, you know the absolute. And even when you have known it, you cannot transform it into a conception.

The whole religious mind has been conceptualizing, but the religious mind means that one has come to know the boundaries of intelligence, the boundaries of intellect, and the boundaries of conceptions. The absolute is beyond, or you can say the beyondness is the absolute. But no conception is possible.

I am not a philosopher, and I deny every type of philosophizing. The truly religious mind is a mind that is not philosophizing about the truth. Philosophizing is a sort of mentation, your mind is working. And through mind, no contact is possible with the absolute. Only when the mind ceases – when thinking ceases, or the ego ceases – do you come in contact with it. But then there is no conception possible. So the absolute must remain beyond conceptions. The absolute must remain beyond "me" and "you."

Where philosophy ends, the absolute begins. Where conceptions end, the absolute begins.

So I have got no conception at all.

Osho,
What do you mean by "me" and "you"?

These are conceptions, egocentric conceptions. When I say "me" and "you," I mean my mental process and your mental process. Unless these processes are... We cannot be in contact with the absolute because these processes are the barrier.

"I" as a thinking mind, is a barrier. "I" as an existential living unit, not a thinking mind, is no barrier. Then there is no "I" and "you"; then the whole existence becomes one.

The ego is "I" and the other ego is the "you." And the absolute comes only when there is egolessness. "I" cannot conceive it, "I" can dissolve in it; "you" can dissolve in it, but "you" cannot conceive it. A drop cannot conceive the ocean. A drop can only conceive the drop. That is its limitation. A drop can become the ocean; it can drop into it and be one with it. Only then it knows – through being, not through thinking. It becomes one with it and knows, but now even this knowing cannot be translated into conceptions.

Conceptions are mental languages – the mind transforming a thing into a thought. I love you: then there is no "I" and there is no "you," but love exists and we both become two polarities of it – two extensions of one feeling, two waves coming and going of one feeling. When you begin to conceive about love, then love becomes a theory, a dead concept – words, principles, philosophies, doctrines – but then there is no love. A theory of love is not love and a theory of godliness is not godliness. The word godliness is not godliness.

So with all these conceptions, I'm not saying this conception is right and that wrong. I'm saying that conceptualization as such is wrong. We cannot conceive. The inconceivable is the absolute. And the moment one begins to think about it, and begins to weave a theory around it, then there are only words and the truth is being lost.

The truth can never become a word.

> Osho,
> What is your attitude towards the Vedic religion, the Vedanta Sutra?

Religion...

> What is the purpose of these literatures if not to discuss the nature of the absolute truth?

It is not...

The absolute truth then is beyond conceptualizing, then how is it then that these literatures such as the Vedanta Sutra and the Bhagavad Gita present description and definition of the absolute truth?

No one presents, no one can present. They all deny, they all deny.

Deny what?

The conceptualization. They all deny conceptualization, and they all propose a living jump into it – not conceiving but a living jump.

And when you say "Vedic religion..." The moment one says Vedic religion, Christian, Hindu, Muslim...the religion is lost. You cannot name it. Religion is religion: it is neither Vedic nor Christian, nor can it be. Religion is not a sect; it is not sectarian. So when you say "Vedic religion," you destroy religion.

Veda means knowledge. Veda means all-knowing.

If you say "all-knowing" then the Bible is the Veda, then the Koran is the Veda. Then there is no need to mention a Vedic religion; then it becomes absurd, irrelevant. If *Veda* means knowledge, then what I am saying, if it is knowledge, is a Veda, and what Mohammed is saying becomes a Veda. Then you cannot use "Vedic religion." When you say "Vedic religion," you mean the knowledge as conceived by the Vedas. Then you confine it; then a sect is being created. And a sectarian mind is not a religious mind; a sectarian mind is basically irreligious.

A mind must endeavor to know, a mind must come to know. The mind must research and seek. But the moment you accept authority, you deny your individuality. That is a suicidal act. The moment you say "Vedic," you have lost something essential for religion.

You may like the Vedas. That is quite another thing. You may love them – that is quite another thing. You may like the Bible, you may love it – that is quite another thing. But don't be bound by it, don't make it a bondage, don't be confined to it – because knowing is such a vast thing that Vedas and Vedas may come and go, and knowing never ends. The Vedas end, but knowing never ends. And knowing is infinite; the Vedas are not infinite. So a person who attaches himself, clings to some particular creed is not a religious person at all.

To me, religion means an attitude toward reality: an attitude of inclusion.

There are three attitudes possible. A scientific mind: a mind which believes in analysis; a mind which believes in objectivity, a mind which believes in experiments, laboratories – not inside but outside – a mind which is concerned with the "without" of things.

And then there is an artistic attitude: a person who is not concerned with reality as truth but reality as feeling; not concerned with the realization of reality but concerned with the expression of it. It is a participatory attitude toward the real, but emotional – a feeling attitude.

And then there is the religious mind – very different, quite different from the scientific mind, because it is not analytical; it synthesizes.

When you say "The Vedas," you become analytical; you have begun to divide religion. Religion is an attitude of synthesis. If you say that The Vedas is all that has been known, then there is no need to mention "the Vedic religion." Then Christ is a Vedic person, then Mohammed is, then Confucius is, then I am and you are. But no, that is not the point. When you say "Vedic" you have confined yourself to a particular scripture. The moment you mention a name, you have become sectarian. And the sectarian mind is so small that it can never be religious. A religious mind must be limitless, untethered to anything, not clinging to anything, not confined to anything.

And when I say "a religious mind," taken as an attitude it means a subjective search for reality, a subjective experimentation with reality, an approach, a seeking – not about the "without" of things but about the "within" of things. And that seeking is subjective, inner. You become concerned with the ultimate, concerned for the ultimate, but you go to it as an individual, not as a member of a sect. You cannot, because the moment you become a member of a particular sect, your mind is burdened with these conceptions, authorities, scriptures. Then you are not fresh, then you are not naked, then you are not innocent. Your mind has become calculating. Now you are not ready to receive truth as it is. Rather, on the contrary, you have your conception of truth to impose on it. Now the truth must come through your scriptures, now the truth must correspond with your conceptions. You are not open.

> *No, just one moment, I did not say anything about my conceptions. I said I am thinking that the truth should correspond with the scriptural conceptions which are not my conceptions.*

The scriptures are not religious. There is no religious scripture at all. Scriptures cannot be religious.

> *Really? I have some verses which conflict with that. I would just like to read them. This is the Bhagavad Gita, Chapter 7, Verse 7. Lord Krishna is speaking to Arjuna. He says: "O character of wealth, Dhananjaya, there is no truth superior to me. Everything rests upon me as pearls are strung on a thread."*
> *And here he is speaking of himself subjectively.*
> *Then in the eighth chapter he is speaking of himself objectively. He says: "Think of the supreme person as one who knows everything; who is the oldest, who is the controller, who is smaller than the smallest, the*

> *maintainer of everything beyond any material conception, inconceivable and always a person. He is luminous like the sun, beyond this material nature, transcendental."*
> *Now in these verses in the Bhagavad Gita, Lord Krishna, who is a person who is standing before Arjuna, speaking to Arjuna, and saying, "Actually I am the absolute truth and there is no truth superior to me and that everything is under my control and that I am a person." And these are the statements of the Bhagavad Gita, which is saying that we can describe what is the absolute truth...*

No. The very statement says it is inconceivable.

> *...or that the absolute truth is describing himself.*

The very statement says it is inconceivable, it is beyond all material conceptions. And the moment you say person you have conceptualized. And if he says...

> *I am not saying "person." That inconceivable lord is revealing knowledge to us and he is saying, "I am a person."*

Then he must mean something other than what we mean by person.

> *But he is not saying, "I mean something else."*

No, no. He is not saying anything at all. He is just saying...

> *Lord Krishna is not speaking in the Bhagavad Gita?*

I won't say "Lord Krishna." That is our conception that he is a lord. And it is our conception that this is a scripture, it is our conception that this is religious, it is our conception that all that is said in it is true. These are our conceptions. And the moment we conceive of a thing as a scripture, then everything becomes authoritatively true, then there is no need to think about it.

What I am saying is this: Truth can be known, but cannot be expressed – not even Krishna can express it. And the moment he expresses it, the truth becomes confined to words, and words come to us, not the truth. If I have known the truth I can try to describe it, but it is never described.

So then what do you do?

I only try to describe the indescribable-ness of it. I only deny the positive formulations. I only try to point out your limitations of knowing, information, scripture, knowledge. And if this much can be pointed out – that our minds are not capable of knowing it – then something is being indicated which is significant. So all that can be done is negative, never positive.

But even a child can know that he has boundaries, so what is the purpose?

No one – not even a child, not even an old man – knows that he has boundaries.

But we all experience boundaries every day...

We experience them, and still we try to conceive the unbound, we try to conceive the absolute, we try to conceive the infinite. And we even try to conceive it through scriptures. Then it becomes absurd. Then it shows that we are not completely aware of our boundaries, the boundaries of our thinking, the boundaries of our thought. We are not aware of them. And the mind feels satisfied if words can be fed to it and if an illusion of knowledge can be created – so I can read the Gita, memorize it, go on continuing to memorize it, and feel that something is being known.

No, nothing is being known. You are just computerizing your mind, you are feeding it with information. The words on the lips of Krishna may have been true – he may have known what he is saying – but the moment it is said, the truth is not conveyed, only the words are conveyed, and we begin to cling to these words. And these words become the base of all our knowledge.

Words can never be a base to knowing. One must go into total silence; one must go into total wordlessness.

> *That is not possible.*

If that is not possible, then absolute truth cannot be known; then you will go on knowing relative conceptions of it.

> *Actually everything you are saying is based on your authority. You are speaking from your authority on this matter.*

How can I speak anything else?

> *Yes, alright, so try and understand like this: that anything that we can say will be based on the authority of these real scriptures.*

That too is your authority. That too is not the authority of the scriptures!

> *I just want to submit then, that since you do not accept these revealed scriptures yourself, you say that they are trying to define something which is undefineable... The scripture has a different opinion. I will just read it. This is in the, um...*

No. I have read them, so you need not trouble yourself.

> *This is just for the presentation of the present moment. Lord Krishna says: "Anyone, therefore, who acts immediately without caring for the regulations of the scriptures can never have perfection in his life, nor happiness nor the supreme destination." He says: "One should understand what is duty and what is not duty by the regulations of the scriptures..."*

So he is exploiting your fear.

> *"...and knowing such rules and regulations one should act so that he may gradually be elevated."*
> *So he is saying that the absolute truth is inconceivable to us in our present conditioned state. And he is also saying that in our present conditioned state...*

I know what he is saying already. I know what he is saying!

> *...if we take action according to his instructions we will gradually be elevated to the point where we can become conscious of the absolute truth by following the regulations of the scriptures.*

The moment you say, "By following the regulations of the scriptures," this is your choice, not Krishna's. You are choosing and you become the authority again.

> *Krishna says, "maam"; Krishna says, er...*

When he says "maam" he doesn't mean Krishna. He means "the inner me" which is in you. It is not concerned with Krishna at all.

> *But he doesn't say that.*

He says, "*Maamekam sharanam vraj*" He says "Come to me, the one." That means the one is within you. It is not concerned with Krishna at all.

> *If I say, if I say "Hand me the microphone, give the microphone to me," and you take the microphone and point it behind me...*

[Osho chuckles.]

> *...then what is the point of my saying, "Give it to me"? Lord Krishna is standing before Arjuna, he is speaking to Arjuna: "Just try and save me and I will elevate you..."*

The person that is standing before him, the person that is seen by Arjuna, is not the real Krishna. The person who is at the same time standing before and behind him is Krishna.

> *And you are saying Krishna's body is immaterial?*

Yes. The material conception of Krishna is not Krishna.

> *We do not say Krishna's body is material...*

Krishna is saying that! I do not know what you are saying.

> *In here it says that Krishna's body is spiritual, transcendental.*

If the body becomes transcendental then it is not the body at all. Then it becomes cosmic. Then there is no body.

> *It says: "Although I am unborn and my transcendental body never deteriorates and although I am the lord of all sentient beings I still appear in every millennium*

> *in my original, transcendental form." My original transcendental form! He says in the seventh chapter of the Bhagavad Gita that...*

This I know already. You need not trouble yourself.

> *Well, you're...*

You need not trouble yourself.

> *How to understand the difference between* saguna *and* nirguna*? What is the meaning of the word* nirguna*. Krishna's uses the word* nirguna*...*

When Krishna uses it, he knows what he is using, but when you imitate it you don't know what you are saying. When he says nirguna then he knows what he means, but when you impose your conception on nirguna it is not. You can only go on repeating it. You can only go on mechanically repeating it.

> *This is not mechanical. This is simply meaning...*

If you have understood it please close this. If you have understood it, please close it. Don't be bothered with it; don't be obsessed with it. If you have not understood it, then you will have to say.

> *But I have understood it. I have understood it and I can paraphrase it...*

Then please close it. There is no need...

> *But it is better to use a direct quotation than to paraphrase. I have not memorized it you see, but I can read it and I can understand what it means and I am simply*

> *presenting this authority in the face of your authority to see whether or not you can explain these* slokas *in such a way...*

No, no. I am not concerned at all in expounding on any *slokas!*

> *"All states of being, be they of goodness, passion or ignorance, are manifested by my energy. I am in one sense everything, but I am independent. I am not under modes of this material nature." Lord Krishna is saying he is not under the mode of this material nature. So what Krishna is saying is that he is not part of this material world. He says in the fourth chapter that his body is transcendental and that it never deteriorates so that he descends on a material planet but then he is always transcendental to this material nature. Shripad Shankarachraya acknowleged that narayana existed before the material creation. And Shripad Shankaracharya's last words to his disciples:* "Bhaj Govindam, Bhaj Govindam, Bhaj Govindam...

This is all nonsense, that the disciples heard this "*Govindam.*" This is all nonsense! Religion is not concerned with these nonsensical things at all.

> *"Just worship Govinda." He said, "You rascals! Just worship Govinda, just worship Govinda, just worship Govinda, because all your nonsense and mental speculation will not help you one minute at the time of your death. You may carry all..."*

There is no death and there is no time of death at all. So there is no question of any help. You cannot die.

> *We are speaking of conditioned souls, because I think, er...*

Even a conditioned soul is not going to die. It may be in the illusion of dying, but no one is dying, so you don't need any help.

> It is this illusion in which we are entangled. Therefore we are looking for that knowledge which will carry us beyond this illusion so that at the time of death we will have something, have developed something, which will free us from the illusion of death and rebirth, so that we can go beyond this repetition of birth and death.

[Osho chuckles.] So you go on becoming...

> So, Shripad Shankaracharya is recommending you simply worship Govinda and then you will transcend this material nature. He says so long as you concern yourself with this er...

This in itself is so material and so mechanical you cannot transcend by it. You can just be auto-hypnotized, that's all.

> You cannot transcend by knowledge, but if you can receive such knowledge that you can act upon it, and you can live that knowledge, and you can put that knowledge into effect every moment...

Knowledge cannot be put into effect. Knowledge comes as an effect. You are not to put it into effect, you are not to make it a reality – it is a reality in itself. You can only be exposed to it; you can only be open to it and you know it. And the moment it is known, you are transformed.

> Lord Krishna says he is the end of all knowledge. He says "By all the Vedas..."

How am I concerned with your Lord Krishna?

> *You are his part and parcel.*

How am I concerned with your Lord Krishna?

> *You are his part and parcel. Lord Krishna says that...*

I am not concerned at all.

> *What? So long as you reject that fact...*

[Osho chuckles.] You may say that I am, but I am not concerned at all. You may say anything.
He is free to say it.

> *He says that "When you have thus known the truth, you will know that all human beings are my parts and parcels. Even if you are considered to be the most simple of all sinners, when you are situated in the boat of transcendental knowledge you will be able to cross over the ocean of miseries."*

[Chuckling again] There are no oceans and no miseries!

> *This is that knowledge by which you can cross over this illusion of the material nature.*

If it is illusion there is no crossing over. And if you cross over it, then it is not illusion, it becomes a reality. If it is illusion then there is no crossing over. You have already crossed.

> *So there is no suffering? There is no misery?*

If it is illusion, then there is no suffering, then there is no misery

– you have crossed. And if it is not illusion, then you will have to cross it. If you cross it, you make it a reality.

If the river is not, no bridge is needed. And if you need a bridge and say the river is illusory, then you will only be creating an illusory bridge: because I am an illusory river no real bridge can be made. So the river is illusory, the bridge is illusory, the passer is illusory, the passing is illusory, and the reaching will be illusory.

> *It may be true that I am dreaming that a tiger is eating me and it is a dream and actually there is no tiger eating me. That may be very true. But as I am dreaming I am suffering intense misery...*

And *bhaj govindam*?

> *...it is causing me very much suffering.*

Then that too is a dream and nothing else. If, in dreaming, the tiger is not, then the *bhaj govindam* is not too.

> *The reason I can dream of the tiger is because somewhere there is the real tiger, and my image of the tiger is only the perverted reflection of that real tiger. What we call knowledge in this material world is not knowledge; it is illusion, but the reason we have the conception of knowledge is because there is real knowledge. That real knowledge is in the spiritual reality from which we have fallen and until we again situate ourselves in our eternal position, our eternal reality, then we will remain in this illusioned condition. And even though we are not actually suffering, by association with this illusory energy, we suffer.*

There is no illusion and no reality. All that is, is.

> *Excuse us. We have to go now.*

12

Right Questioning

BEFORE YOU ASK SOMETHING, I MUST TELL YOU that there are two types of questioning. One type of questioning comes, not because you do not know, but because you know something. It comes out of your so-called knowledge. You have the answer already and then you raise the question. It shows two things.

Whatsoever you know, you have not really known it; otherwise there would have been no question. And secondly, because the question has been raised by our preconceived conditioning, by our preconceived answer, you are not even ready to receive a new answer. So whenever there is such questioning it is absolutely useless. It leads you nowhere.

Never ask because you know something. If you know, it is good. Then there is no need of asking. If you don't know, then ask as if you are ignorant, you don't know - because unless you feel that you don't know, you are never vulnerable, open, receptive. And receptivity is needed otherwise you raise a question and don't allow the answer to go in. But all questions are more or less like that. We have the answer already and then we question.

This is really a search for confirmation. You are not confident because really you don't know; you have simply gathered some information. Now you want someone to give you conviction, recognition. You want someone to be a witness to your knowledge, so that you can feel, "Yes, I am right."

This is very absurd. If you know, then knowledge itself, knowing itself, gives the confidence, the conviction. It is self-evident,

RIGHT QUESTIONING

always self-evident. If you know something, then even if the whole world denies it, it makes no difference. In just the same way, if you don't know a thing and the whole world says, "Yes, this is right," it too makes no difference. Knowing is self-evident and ignorance is also self-revealing.

So don't ask from your knowledge. If you know, it is good. If you don't know, then be conscious that you don't know and ask from your conscious ignorance.

The second type of questioning, which is authentic questioning, inquiry – sincere, honest – is always from the feeling that you do not know. And the moment that you feel you don't know, your doors are open. Now, you are ready to invite the guest. Otherwise you invite the guest and your house is completely closed. Then don't invite! If you invite, then make a space for the guest. If you have ready-made answers, then you have no space within you. You can ask questions, but then you have no space within you to receive answers.

Questioning is useless if there is no space to receive. So see when you are asking: is there any space to receive an answer? First create the space, then ask. Then, this second type of questioning becomes existential, then it is not merely intellectual, then it is not merely mental. You are totally involved in it; your whole is at stake, your total being. This is what is meant by "being existential." Now it comes from your very existence, from your very being.

The first type of questioning is always conditioned by others. This must be understood very clearly. Ignorance is yours, and your so-called knowledge is given by others. Ignorance is more existential than so-called knowledge. If you don't know, this not knowing is yours. And if you say, "I know because I have read the Gita," this knowing is not yours. "I know because so-and-so has said such and such a thing, because Buddha had such knowledge and I have become acquainted with it, therefore, I know" – this knowledge is not yours

And remember, even your ignorance is more valuable than

THE ETERNAL QUEST

others' knowledge. At least it is yours. Something can be done with it. It is real, existential. Nothing can be done with a fiction. The real can be transformed and changed, but with the fiction you can do nothing, with imagination you can do nothing. Imagined knowledge, based only on information, is fictitious. It is not existential.

So ask a question, inquire about something, through your existential feelings, not your accumulated, mental information. If you really ask from your ignorance, then your question will be universal in one way and individual in another way – individual and at the same time universal – because when you ask from your ignorance the problem is the same for everyone, but if you ask from your knowledge, then the problem differs.

A Hindu may never ask a question which a Mohammedan can ask; a Christian will never ask the same question that a Jaina asks, because a Mohammedan's knowledge is completely different from a Christian's knowledge – though there is Mohammedan ignorance and no Hindu ignorance. Ignorance is universal, existential. Mohammedan knowledge is different from Hindu knowledge, Buddhist knowledge is different from Jaina knowledge, and if your questioning is raised by your knowledge, it is bound to social – just racial conditioning, and not universal, existential.

So when a Mohammedan asks something, he is not really asking, but that which has been put into him is asking, that which has been forced upon him, imposed upon him – that which has been conditioned. That conditioning is asking; the real man is behind it. The Mohammedan, the imposed Mohammedan or the imposed Hindu, is asking. Then it is superficial, and whatsoever answer is given is not going to penetrate to your depths because the question was never from the depths.

Existential questioning means you go to your depths through all the conditioning layers of your mind and ask, just as a pure, bare existence – not as a Mohammedan, Hindu, Sikh, Jaina... Ask as if you have not been given any answers before. Put your answers aside. Then, your question will be individual in one way, because it has come from you, and simultaneously universal, because whenever someone goes inside to such a depth, the same question will come.

So be existential in asking, and never ask from your knowledge. Ask from your ignorance. If you want transformation, mutation, then ask from your ignorance. Be aware of your ignorance. Dig deep and find the questioning which is coming out of your ignorance, not out of your knowledge. Only then are you aware of your basic difficulty.

So now, ask!

Osho,
Is it not true that answers have been given through God without the question being raised? Even though I have never asked a question, the answers have been given before the question arose in me.

In a way it is both correct and incorrect.

Questions have been raised; otherwise answers would not be possible. It may be that you have not raised the question. Someone raised it, and the first time, the question was raised from ignorance and the answer was given by a person from knowing.

But then everything becomes formulated. From then on, the question becomes formulated, the answer becomes formulated. Then we have ready-made questions and ready-made answers.

And because every child is going to ask the same questions really – because existence is the same and the problem is the same, and to pass through existence is to pass through the same suffering and the same inquiry – just as a safety measure, parents and teachers give answers before the question is raised. Neither is the question raised, nor does the giver know the answer. Both have become traditional.

Because we know that the question is bound to come, before

it comes…because once it comes, you will not be able to impose any answer. Once a real question comes into being, then the society, the establishment, the father, the mother, the teacher, will not be able to impose an answer, because a real question is so powerful that your bogus answers will not do. So it is just a safety measure: before someone asks, give him an answer. Then the real question will never be raised, will never come into being, because when you have given an answer, planted a false answer, the person will continue to ask questions about this answer, not about the basic point. He will go on asking.

You have planted an answer that there is a God and he has created the world. The child never asked you; you have given an answer. Now this answer will go deep, because you have planted this answer in such a moment when the child was not even aware of the question. He was not aware really of existential problems.

So it will be deep in the mind and when the child comes to question things, this answer will have become his unconscious layer. Now, he will not ask whether the world has been created or not. He will ask, "If God has created this world, then why is there evil?"

This is a secondary question. This is not authentic, existential. This is because of that answer – the answer is already there that God has created the world. Now the problem arises. If God has created the world – it is taken for granted that God has created the world – then why is there evil? This "why is there evil?" is a question because of the answer.

And there are layers and layers. You can answer even this question before the child becomes aware. Then, on the third round, he will raise questions.

Then, on the third round he will raise questions. And the more sophisticated a society is, the more far away the questioning goes from an existential one. Really, a sophisticated society, a cultured society, means so many answers are given already for which there was no question.

RIGHT QUESTIONING

And one has to begin from the beginning. That's why I insist that your answers must be thrown away; otherwise you will continue to ask questions that are not basic, not foundational, but only secondary – because of the answers that are already implanted.

So I say that it is both correct and incorrect, because if there is no question, no answer is possible. So when a question comes into the world for the first time, it always comes through existential inquiry. For a Buddha the question is existential, but for a Buddhist it is not. For a Buddha, it is not through his conditioning. He has thrown it. He has raised basic questions, and now he goes in search, and then there is an answer, he comes to know something. His answer is authentic because it has come through authentic questioning.

But this answer will be given to others. They may not be in the least interested in the basic question, but they will take this answer because it becomes an accumulation, it makes them richer – at least it makes them feel richer.

You also know: you accumulate answers, many answers. And then these answers are being transferred from generation to generation. Every generation goes on adding, because every generation asks some existential questions and gets some existential knowing. These answers are being added.

So the more cultured a society is, the greater the accumulated heritage of answers, and the less is the possibility of your being in the situation where you can ask a basic question. And if you cannot ask one, then you cannot receive a basic answer. Your questioning is false; you will continue getting false answers.

So first be aware, so that your question is not coming from some answer implanted in you. Put aside the answer. Ask something that is existential to you. If nothing was taught to you – if no answer was given – no theory, no system, no religion – then would there have been any question or not? If there can be a questioning, only that questioning is existential, basic, religious.

So put aside all the conditioned answers and dig deep, to the original being, and face life from there. There will be questions – alive. You may even find it difficult how to formulate them, how to put them, how to ask them, because you have never asked a fundamental question, so you don't know how to ask. It is better not to ask. Suffer. It is better to suffer that "I cannot ask" than to ask unnecessary things, because through this suffering, you will be able, you will be able to ask. And the moment you are able to ask, you are ready to be given to, because the same process through which you become capable of asking a foundational question, that same process is needed for a foundational answer to penetrate in you, and that same path will be used.

If you go deeply into yourself to find a real question, you create a passage in you. That same passage can be used by me. If there is no passage in you, my answer cannot penetrate you more deeply than that from where your question has come. The layer of penetration will be the same. If your question is superficial, then any answer will just become a superficial thing to you.

Sometimes it has happened that the questioner was authentic and the teacher was not. Sometimes it has happened that the questioner was authentic and the teacher was not, but still the questioner could get the answer. The other way around has never happened: when the teacher is authentic but the questioner is not authentic, then nothing can be done.

Even a false teacher will do, because really the work is being done by you, not by a teacher. So even a stone image will do; if you are really concerned, then a stone image will give you the answer. And if you are not really concerned, then a living Buddha is dead, meaningless – because ultimately, it depends on you. It depends not on the teacher, it depends on the disciple, it depends on the questioner.

If you can ask a foundational question from the very heart of your being, the answer will come to you even if there is no one there – the vacuum will create the answer, existence itself will give you the answer. But with false questioning, nothing is possible and nothing can be done.

So try to formulate. Even if you fail in your effort, it is good. Try to formulate some problem which comes from you, not from the society, not from your teachers, not from your upbringing – just from you.

This is a meditation. This finding out is a meditation. So find some question!

13

Beyond Polarities, Beyond Time

Osho,
There is a great sense of weakness and helplessness. Where is one to find strength from? The moments of realness are very small and the burden of habits is so great.

REALLY, IT IS NOT LIKE THIS. It is not that you feel helpless and weak because you don't have strength. You feel weak because there is a craving for more strength. It is comparative, it is relative.

It is not that you are weak. You are as you are, neither weak nor strong. But there is a craving to be stronger, to be more – in any dimension. That craving creates comparison, and that craving will continue within you. So wherever you are, howsoever strong, it makes no difference. You will feel weak because your craving will have grown further. There will be this distance, the same distance, and you will feel weak and helpless.

So one has to understand why you feel weak. You feel weak because you create an image of strength. You create an end and put it somewhere in the future. Then you feel weak.

This weakness is just your creation. And it makes no difference – even if you are made the whole and soul in this universe, even if you are a god, it will make no difference. You will create the same distinction; the same distance will be created. You will feel weak because the same mind will be there; it will again project a better situation. The mind can always project and imagine a better situation. No situation is such that you cannot imagine a better one. You can always imagine a better one, and if you can imagine a better one, you will feel weak.

So what to do? There have been teachers who say. "Don't look into the future. Look in the past." They say: "If you want to feel strong, don't create an image of strength but look back and see how weak you were. Then you will feel strong."

But the fallacy is the same and the foolishness is the same. It makes no difference, no difference. If you feel strong in comparison to some weak image about your own past or of some other's, it will be impossible to escape the future. If you create this, you will create the other. There is another pole of it; you cannot escape it. So as far as I am concerned, I see that whatsoever you are, you can neither be more nor less at this moment – whatsoever you are, X, Y, Z; whatsoever you are. In this moment, the whole universe, the whole of existence, has culminated in you as you are.

If you go just anywhere from this point, you will create misery for yourself. Remain with this facticity of your being: you are this. "This is the fact, and I don't create any image to be compared with. This is the fact; I am this. I am angry, I am anger. This is the fact. At this moment, this is the truth. And if I am ready and daring and courageous enough to be with the fact, then there is no weakness, and no helplessness at all."

I am not going to say that you will feel strong. I am not going to say that. You will feel neither strong nor weak. And that is the moment of freedom. When you are neither weak nor strong, you just are – because when you are strong, the same process continues. More will be asked. If you are weak, more will be asked. It makes no difference; the difference is only of degrees.

Whatsoever you are at this moment, be with it. Don't escape in imagination. Then there is no helplessness, then there is no weakness, then there is no strength. And when there is no comparison, you are authentically yourself. There is no condemnation either, no appreciation either: you are, and there is a *total* acceptance, a total acceptance.

THE ETERNAL QUEST

And when one accepts oneself totally, one accepts the whole of existence. Unless you can accept yourself, you will never be able to accept anyone. It is impossible for one who cannot accept himself to accept anyone. And then the whole misery follows.

You love someone, and you cannot accept him: he could be more lovely, he could be more beautiful, he could be more healthy. The "more" will follow, and with the "more" you will condemn that which is; you are bound to condemn it.

You cannot love because love requires total acceptance. You cannot accept yourself, so how can you accept anyone else? Impossible! And this non-acceptance, this constant denial, creates misery.

Wherever you are, you are unhappy – not because there is any fixed destiny for you to be unhappy; it is only because you have been playing with the faculty of the mind which imagines, and not with the faculty of the mind which remains with the fact. Mind has both faculties. Imagination is needed. It helps in many ways; it creates all the dimensions of discovery. Use it there, invent through it. But it is a misused, misdirected imagination if you begin to deny the fact and create a fiction. Then you will miss existence completely, constantly, continuously.

So you feel weak, one feels weak and helpless, because one has an image. That is your creation. Destroy the image and be with the fact. Then there is an explosion. You feel neither weak nor strong. You just feel you are, and there is a freedom from relativity, from comparison. And once you are free from comparing yourself with your own images, you will never compare yourself with anyone, because he is he and you are you and every comparison is nonsense. Then there is a total acceptance of all that is. In this total acceptance is the ecstasy of life. Then, moment to moment you live it and feel the bliss of it.

So it is not about how to be strong, it is about how to be free from this craving. Why this craving? Why does one want to be something other than how one is? Why is there this craving to be something else, to be someone else, to be somewhere else? Why?

BEYOND POLARITIES, BEYOND TIME

If you go deep inside, you will come to know and understand that this constant craving to be somewhere else is because you have not yet learned how to be there, where you are. You have not gone through a discipline – if I may use the word – through the learning of how to be there, where you are. You know only one thing: never to be there, where you are; always to be somewhere else.

Why? Why is this? If you can be somewhere where you are not, why can't you be there, where you are? You are trying a more difficult, a rather impossible thing, so why not try the possible, the only possible thing? Why? The mind has a trick, and a very cunning trick. It has proven very useful, so it goes on using it. To be there, where you are, is to face reality. There will be problems. To be where you are not is to go on dreaming; there will be no problems. So it is just intoxicating – just intoxicating!

If you love a woman and remain with her, it is going to create problems. But if you imagine a woman and live with her, it is going to create no problems at all. You are alone. There is no one to create problems. So it is intoxicating to create dreams, because then you are the God amidst your dreams. This is your world.

The real world is not yours, rather, on the contrary, you are part of the real world, just a minute part, just an atomic quanta – really, nothing.

What am I in the real world? Nothing! But in my imaginary world, I am divine, I am the whole and soul. The dreams are mine; the whole dreamy world is mine. I may do whatsoever I like. So the mind takes on the trick, and whenever there is difficulty in the real world, you escape into the dream. You learn the trick. And every moment there is difficulty in the real world – there is bound to be – the mind goes on continually escaping somewhere else.

This is the reason why there is this craving. Understand this, be aware of this, and by and by, whenever you feel that you are creating a dream again, just be aware, and the dream will wither away and you will be thrown back to reality.

THE ETERNAL QUEST

Howsoever painful, be with the reality. Howsoever pleasant, don't be with the dreams. They are pleasant – that's why we are with them. And reality is not pleasant. But through pleasant dreams, you are never going to get any bliss. Only through painful reality does one reach the blissful moment. If you want real bliss, you will have to pass through real pain, real suffering. That is the price to be paid.

If you don't pay the price, then you can continue dreaming, Really, you are paying more – and for nothing. In this way, you are not escaping reality, you are just thinking that you are escaping. You are going to suffer, you *will* continue suffering. The reality will be there, and the suffering will be there, and the pain will be there, only you will have morphia with you, opium with you.

The human mind has always longed for intoxicating drugs. They are chemical ways to escape. They are just mental ways to escape. Everyone begins to.

You will be surprised that the more aboriginal races, the more primitive races, don't dream much. A dreamer is really a phenomenon. In a primitive community, one who dreams becomes a prophet, because ordinarily there is no dreaming. They live so much with reality that dreaming is not needed.

The more cultured a society, the more dreaming there is. And then, in the end, the night is not enough. You have to dream in the daytime also. Then there is a continuous circle of dreaming inside. Sometimes you are dreaming less, sometimes more – that is the only difference.

But if you just penetrate inside, you will see a film of dreams continuously going on. Just close your eyes and there is a dream. It is not that you had your eyes open so a dream was not there. It was there, running, but you were not there to see it, that's the only thing. Close your eyes, relax, and the dream is there, just waiting for you to continue. It is there, waiting for you.

This dreaming mind is the reason. It goes on creating better images. And then there is comparison, then there is misery – you feel weak. This weakness is created by our minds. Otherwise no one is weak and no one is strong. Everyone is as he is. Each individual is so individual that comparison is impossible. How can you compare?

Ordinarily, you will not compare yourself with a stone. You will not compare, because a stone is a stone. But if you are a man, you will compare yourself with a man. Why? – because you feel that "We are alike." You will not compare yourself with a woman, because the whole culture has trained your mind so that there is no reason to compare yourself with a woman. You are a man, so you compare yourself with a man because you are alike.

We compare only when we feel alike. No one will say that "This tree is more beautiful than my wife." It is meaningless. And if you say it, then the wife is not going to be violent about it. She will just laugh. But tell her, "That woman is more beautiful" and it becomes misery.

The whole attitude of comparison is based on the feeling of alikeness. But no one is alike. It is not that one man and another man can be compared – no. They cannot be compared. They are so absolutely different – more different than a tree and a woman. Nothing is alike; every existence is unique. But this uniqueness can only be felt when you don't escape into dreaming.

Be with the facts and you will come to know that everyone is unique, not that you are unique. If you feel, "I am unique," you are still in comparison, because this uniqueness is that in comparison to someone else, "I am unique." If someone says, "I am unique," then it is still a comparison. When you feel that everyone is unique, every moment of time, every stone, every tree, every leaf of a tree is unique...

This uniqueness is felt when you live with your facticity. Then this uniqueness is revealed to you; then there is no comparison. Then you never feel weak or strong, foolish or wise, beautiful or ugly, because there is nothing to compare with. You are alone.

Think. This whole attitude: if everyone dies and only you

have remained on the earth, will you feel foolish or wise, beautiful or ugly? If you are alone, then there is no question: you are the same as you were with others. You are the same, but because there is no comparison you cannot say, "I am wise."

If you live with your facticity, with your being as it is, you become alone amidst the crowd. One comes to be just an island, alone, and there is no one to be compared with. All comparison falls. And then you have a freedom – completely unknown.

In that freedom, you are to be whatsoever you are. And that is the only freedom I know of: to be whatsoever you are. Otherwise there is misery – layers and layers of misery and worlds and worlds of hell that you go on creating continuously.

Everyone lives in a multidimensional hell, because it is not only in one dimension that we compare; we continually compare in multi-dimensions. Someone is more healthy, someone is more beautiful, someone is more wise, someone is more strong, someone is more wealthy – multi-dimensions of comparison. And everyone comparing with everyone else lives in a multidimensional hell. Everywhere is hell!

The mind is such that no one can come out of this comparison to any heaven, to any blissful state of mind – not even an emperor. He has everything, the whole world in his hands, and a beggar just passes by his side, singing, and he feels miserable. He cannot sing like that. The whole kingdom, the whole wealth, and the whole victory have become useless. Just a beggar singing by the corner of the road, and the emperor is no longer an emperor; he has become miserable. He cannot sing like that! The same mind, in any situation, will create, through different routes...

So be with the fact. Don't ask how to be stronger, what is the method to be stronger, how not to feel helpless. If you are helpless, then feel helpless. Why create the other? If I am helpless, I must feel helplessness. And this is the miracle: if I can be at ease with my helplessness, I am no longer helpless – because I am helpless, and the sting is because I don't want to be. If I am ready to accept that I am helpless, if I am ready to live with this helplessness, then where is the helplessness? It has gone. Now I can never feel helpless.

This is the dynamic of the mind: if you feel helplessness, and endeavor to reach a point against it, you are never going to be beyond it. Don't endeavor to be what is against it, what is the opposite. Just be, and it withers away; it is found nowhere. It is found only in the opposite – and it is the mind that creates the opposite. It says, "This is not good. Be like that." See the mechanism, and the stupidity of it. I am helpless, I am weak. My mind says, "Be strong." How can a weak man be strong? And if I can be strong, then I am not weak.

I am weak. My mind says, "You are weak. Now find some way to be strong." How can I find a way? How can I be strong when I am weak, and how can strength be achieved through weakness? I will have to endeavor; the weak, the weakness, will endeavor to be strong. But how? It is impossible. I am helpless, I am ignorant, and the ignorance tries to be knowledge. How can ignorance be knowledge?

Look at it in this way. A madman is trying not to be mad. He will be more mad, because how can a madman try not to be mad? It is better to be mad, because then at least the madness is of a single round. If he tries not to be mad, the madness is doubled, because it is the madness that will be trying, and if madness can try not to be mad, then anything is possible in the world.

But this is the case with all of us. Weakness trying to be strong, ignorance trying to be wisdom, ugliness trying to be beautiful – everyone trying for the opposite and knowing very well that, "I am weak." If we can be aware of this phenomenon, then if I am weak, I am weak, and there is nowhere to go. I accept it; I don't try for the opposite. It is a fact: I am weak.

Accept it, with no struggle for the opposite. And the moment there is no struggle, are you weak? Can you say you are weak? The moment the struggle drops, you are not weak.

Create the opposite and you will remain the same. Accept the same, and you are transformed. This is the contradiction of all mysticism. Socrates says: "People call me wise because I am the only one who has become aware of his ignorance." Lao Tzu says: "You cannot defeat me because I am already defeated. No one can defeat me. My victory is settled because I have accepted defeat."

Come and defeat me. You will not have to endeavor; you will feel I am already defeated, so how can you defeat me? You can only have the pleasure of defeating me if I struggle with you. If I just lie down and request of you, "Just come and sit on me. I am defeated, be victorious!" then you will just look childish. You will look childish, and foolish, because the whole pleasure of victory is in the fighting, in subduing someone. But one is already subdued.

There is a saying of Mansoor: "Death is impossible for me, because I have accepted it." It will be so, it is so. Death exists in your fear of death. It cannot exist if you accept it, if you are ready to meet and invite and embrace it.

This is the reason why the Upanishads speak in paradoxes. They say: "If you want to enjoy, renounce." You cannot conceive the other part, but the opposite must not be denied. Somewhere, it must be accepted and assimilated. You mustn't be against it; you must create a space within you in which the opposite is also accepted. Then they both negate each other and you are free. Weakness denied creates the concept, the image, of strength. When weakness is accepted then there is no opposite.

Can you imagine one who accepts weakness not accepting strength? One who accepts death obviously accepts life. One who accepts unhappiness accepts happiness – there is no question. That's why there is so much emphasis on the negatives – because if you can accept the negative, the positive is already accepted. Both accepted, they negate each other. Strength and weakness negate each other, and you are free from the opposite, from the dual structure of existence. And that is the only freedom. And if you don't mind, freedom is strength, incomparable – not comparing with anyone. It is intrinsic power, energy – infinite.

But through opposites we never fall upon ourselves. We go on continuously choosing the opposite. And see the mystery: those who become powerful, begin to seek weakness. Those who become powerful ultimately begin to seek weakness. A Buddha, renouncing his empire: what is he seeking? What is he going to get? A son of an emperor seeking to be a beggar: what he is seeking, what is his search? He has known power, strength. He has known power, strength, and was frustrated. Now, the opposite: now he will go like a beggar. Again the opposite!

This always happens. Affluence has come to the West for the first time in history. Then their sons and daughters will be hippies, seeking the opposite. Rockefellers and Morgans cannot even conceive that their whole effort to create so much wealth is just going to create an alternative community of beggars. Why? The mind seeks the opposite. It is not that you seek strength when you are weak. When you get strength, you will begin to seek weakness, and you will begin to create illusions about weakness just as you are now creating illusions about strength.

If whatsoever you ask for can be given this very moment, then the second moment you are repulsed. But it is not given, that is the reason we continue asking in our dreams. Get the one you love, and love withers. Get the state you seek, and you begin to ask for the opposite. So it is not only that there is a craving for strength from weakness. When the strength is there, you begin to feel the beauty of weakness. The mind begins to interpret "the bliss of begging." No beggar has ever known any bliss, but emperors have known it when they became beggars. This is a miracle, it is really a miracle! No beggar has known it; he has only known misery and more misery. But Buddha has known it, Mahavira has known it. When they became just beggars they knew it.

So is bliss in begging? It cannot be, because there are beggars,

THE ETERNAL QUEST

they have always been there, but they have never known it. They cannot believe that this is even possible: that Buddha became blissful just by becoming a beggar. How is it possible? The beggar cannot conceive this because he has not known the other pole. From that pole, things begin to be different.

Someone asks Mulla Nasrudin, "Is your house on the left side of the road or on the right?"

Nasrudin closes his eyes, goes into deep meditation, contemplates, and then says, "Sometimes it is on the right and sometimes it is on the left. It depends. When I go from here, it is on the left. When I come from that side, it is on the right. So it changes sides. I have seen it changing sides."

Where is bliss? On the left, on the right? In weakness, in strength? In begging or in kingdoms? Where is it? It depends on where you are coming from. And I have seen it changing places: sometimes it is on the left, sometimes on the right!

Mulla is walking on a street. He asks a man, "Where is the other side of the road?"

The man says. "Are you a fool? That is the other side of the road."

Mulla says. "This is very surprising. When I was on that side, someone said the other side is here. Either I am a fool, or this whole city is crazy! And I have asked so many people. When I am on that side, they say the other side is here. When I come to this side, you say the other side is there. So where is the other side?"

The other side cannot be found. The moment you are on the other side it is not the other side, and you begin to have illusions about the other side which is not there. You cannot have illusions about the fact. You can have only illusions about the fiction. The other side is always the fiction. Somewhere, far off,

BEYOND POLARITIES, BEYOND TIME

dreams are possible. You can project. But they are never on this side.

If you become aware of both sides, you transcend. Then there is no "other side." Then you just drop asking, "Where is the other side?" It is where you are just now. In that transcendence of duality, of sides, of opposites, is freedom – total freedom, infinite freedom. And with infinite freedom, there is infinite energy.

So it is not that knowledge can be gained against ignorance, no. If you gain knowledge against ignorance, it will just be a camouflage, it will just be a covering to hide something. The ignorance will be inside; you will create just a covering of knowledge.

Knowing is when there is neither knowledge nor ignorance – neither side. So I would prefer Socrates to know something more. He says, "People call me wise because I have become aware of my ignorance." He has left one side – the side which claims knowledge. He has come to the other side which claims ignorance. He will have to leave this side also. He can only be perfectly wise if he can say, "I am neither. I have known both, and I am neither. I have been to both sides and I am neither. Neither am I ignorant nor am I wise."

It is very easy to transfer your mind to the opposite and stick to it, but both sides must fall down. Then there arises that consciousness which is, which is really you. That is the third, or the one beyond the two. But one has to pass through, and one has to suffer, and one has to go to the extremes.

Go, not asking for the other, remaining with the one you are at this moment. Sometimes you *will* be the other, but learn the method of being with that which is just now. You will be on the other side soon, so don't bother about it. When you are there, be there. When you are here, be here. Don't bother about it just now, because then you will be missing something which has to be learned. And if you cannot learn it just here, when you are on the other side the same mind will be there. You will be somewhere else again and again and again.

Do not ask for the opposite. And when I say do not ask for the opposite, I don't mean suppress the opposite, because if you suppress, you have already asked. Just be aware of this dualism of the mind, the dynamics of the mind, that the mind works in this way. Just be aware, that's all. You are feeling weak: be weakness, wholeheartedly. You feel ignorant: be ignorant, wholeheartedly. This is how existence happens to be in you – ignorant. This is how existence happens to be in you – weak. This is how existence, destiny, is in you as you are. What can you do? Who are you to do? You are that which you are, so don't divide yourself.

But we are dividing. When I say, "There is anger, it should not be there; there is violence, it should not be there," who is dividing whom? I am anger and in thought I divide myself in two. I say that I am someone else – some supreme self, some superconscious being – and this anger is there just like a disease, and it should not be.

When you are angry, find out if there are two: the angry one and the anger. Never think afterwards. Then there are two, because by then anger has become part of memory; it is a dead thing. When you are angry, just close your eyes and see whether there is someone angry, or if you are simply anger – just energy that has become anger. Is there someone who is above the anger, beyond the anger, different from the anger?

Don't stick to ready-made answers, with a, "Yes, there is soul, there is self, there is a witnessing self which is different." Experiment. When you are in anger, know, there. Is there something that is beyond anger? If you find something, then you will not find anger. If you find something which is beyond, then you will not find anger. If you find anger, then you will not find the beyond.

So what does it mean? It means there is only one: if it is anger then the beyond is not; if it is beyond, then the anger is not. It is the same energy; one energy transforming itself in many ways. When it is anger, then there is nothing left behind. You are

BEYOND POLARITIES, BEYOND TIME

totally angry. If you are witnessing, then nothing is left to be angry: you are a witnessing soul.

But in memory, retrospectively, you can make two. You have been sometimes angry and sometimes not, so you think, "I am two. There is a part, a lower self – something to be condemned and discarded – and there is something higher, supreme, higher, which is to be saved and made free. This misconception comes to you retrospectively when you think about anger. It is not there now. It has become just a memory. Anger is memory; your non-anger states are memory. You can divide them, you can contrast them, you can make them opposites, and now you can choose now which to be. But you are falling into a very pseudo phenomenon.

When you are in love, find out if there is any lover, or only love, energy transformed into love. You will never find any lover, and if you can find any lover, there will be no love. If you can find, "Yes, I am the lover," then there is no love at all. You will not find even the ashes of love; nothing will be left, not even smoke. The lover will be there but then there will be no love. If you find love, then you can keep trying to find the lover, but you will not find the lover at all, because love is the whole energy. Only in memory are you a lover. In fact, in real action, you are love.

So if I am weakness, I must find out if is there someone beyond this weakness who says, "Be strong." No. If you seek, search within, there is weakness but no one who is weak and no one who is beyond weakness.

And if you find that one who is beyond, then there is no weakness. They never coexist. But they coexist in memory, and the whole of human ignorance continues because of memory. All teachings are bound to be based on memory, because teaching is really a memory carried over by the society. Scriptures are memory. That's why we call them *smriti* or we call them *shruti*. *Smriti* means that which has been memorized through the ages, and *shruti* means that which has been heard. They both mean the same: *smriti* on the part of who relates and *shruti* on the part of who listens. So the whole of teaching is memory.

So scriptures will divide you in two. They will say, "Don't be angry!" But this sentence is very false. It says you are something different from anger: "Don't be angry!" This creates duality. Then you begin to think, "'Don't be angry!' How not to be angry? How not to be helpless? How not to be weak? 'Don't be weak!'" But the secret is, if you want to follow this instruction, this injunction of "Don't be weak!" accept weakness, and you will not be. "Don't be angry!" – then *be* totally angry and be aware that you are not there. This awareness has such intensity – only one point more – this awareness has such intensity, it transforms the whole thing.

Physicists say that even atomic particles behave differently when observed. It is possible, and sooner or later will be proved, that when you are looking at a tree it behaves differently because the observer becomes a part of the phenomenon. It behaves differently because you have become part of it. If atomic particles behave differently when observed, then... They go zigzag; they change their route when observed. It seems they feel someone has been observing them.

It is just like when you are passing down a lonely street. No one is there. And then someone leans out of his window and you are different. You may not even be aware that you have become different, but those two eyes observing from the window have become part of you. You cannot be the same; you have become different, the whole situation has become different. Two more eyes – a consciousness aware of you, conscious about you – and something becomes different in you.

This also happens when there is outward observance. That's why everyone talks, everyone speaks, but if you are put on a pedestal and a crowd is there to listen to you, something changes in you: you cannot talk. Why? You have been talking your whole life, you have never felt any difficulty. But what has happened? A crowd of eyes observing you, and you are not the same. So much observation! Something has changed within you; you are different. You don't find anything coming in your mind. It has become vacant.

Observation changes that which is observed. If you can observe your anger, it has a mutative effect. It changes the whole thing. If you observe your anger, there is a mutation, there is a sudden change: there is no anger; you are there. You will not both meet together.

So whatsoever the state of affairs is, be with it, observe it. Don't go into imagination.

Mind has two faculties: imagination and observation. Ordinarily we use only one faculty: imagination. That is the only difficulty for us, the only problem-creating faculty with us. And it has become completely unbalanced. It has gone insane, it will go insane. It must be balanced by observation.

If you are an observer, you can let your freedom go completely. Then it cannot create any problem for you, it will be creative and helpful. But the observer must be there. If the observer is not there and only imagination is there, then you are bound to get into unnecessary difficulties and problems, complexities and conflicts. So bring the observer in, and by the very presence of the observer, the very nature of imagination changes.

Right now it is destructive. Comparison is destructive, it is violence. Right now it is destructive, only creating images to condemn you. Imagination changes its nature when it is with the observer. It becomes creative. Then it is not creating images in the future. Then it becomes a help toward observation.

Life is so rich, but we have never known it. If you observe it with a very imaginative mind, with a very sensitive mind, with a very creative mind, things have a beauty which we have never known. A very ordinary flower becomes something supreme, becomes something ultimate. Observation must be there, total observation, then the very faculty of imagination can begin to work with the observation, to penetrate more and more, to dig more and more – not into the future, but just in the here and now.

It has the power to go somewhere. If you just allow it to go into the future, it will go to moons and to planets, to stars – anywhere. This is one dimension. I would like to call it the dimension of time.

Our imagination travels only one dimension: the dimension of time. It goes either into the future or into the past. It moves in time. With observation there is a change, and imagination begins to move in space, not in time. That is the qualitative change that observation creates. The arrow of imagination moves from "there and then" to "here and now." Space is always here and now; it has no time expansion.

Imagination has two dimensions to develop. Without observation it goes from past to future, from future to past. With observation, it goes into space. Then if you look at a flower...

But if you look at a flower now, the moment you look at the flower, all the flowers and associated things you have ever seen will come into your imagination. You have seen this flower once before, in someone's garden, and all the associations will come in. You are not really seeing this flower. You are seeing a whole series of past flowers associated with it. This flower will just be hidden in so many flowers. If you say "How beautiful!" you are not saying it to this flower. You are saying it to so many associations which have created a feeling and memory that this flower is beautiful. Your imagination has gone into time. It may go into the future, it may say, "A more beautiful flower is possible. This is nothing! Much is possible. With some labor and effort, a bigger flower is possible – more beautiful, with more colors, more alive." Now you have gone into the future, you are not with this flower which exists at the crossroads of future and past. You just bypass it. Either you go to the past or to the future.

With observation, imagination goes deep into this flower, this very flower, this fact. And this flower has a depth which we have not known because we travel in time, and time cannot touch the depth – it is spatial, the depth is in space. So if time is dropped... And observation drops time. You cannot observe a future event, you cannot observe a past event – you can observe only that which is present.

Observation is anti-temporal. It drops time completely. There is only space to move in now, infinite space. A very small flower has infinite space in it. Now move into it. Now you are entering; the flower is just a door and now you are entering the whole existence. The flower becomes just a symbol, just a beginning, just a starter. And then you go deep – in space, not into time. Then, the flower has all in it. That gives you a creative imagination, and with that imagination, one penetrates deep into existence. Then, everything has a depth.

We never penetrate the depth, not even with persons. If you love someone, you are with him, but you are remembering the love that has passed or you are imagining the love that is going to be. But you never move in the space in which the person is, here and now. The person is a space. I will not say "has a space"; the person is a space, a universe to move in.

But you are not moving in it. You have the hand of your beloved or your lover, but the hand has gone dead. You are not there. You are thinking of events from the past, you are imagining things for the future. And the space which you call your lover or beloved is here, the door is just nearby. If you can move into that space, through your lover, you reach to the ultimate of existence.

The ultimate can be found through anything, just the movement should not be in time, the movement should be in space. And that movement of imagination comes with observation.

Enough for today.

14

Suffering: Broken Harmony

Osho,
In both the Eastern and the Western hemispheres, in every dimension of life, people are suffering. Will you diagnose this suffering for us: its causes, its preventions and its cures?

SUFFERING IS SYMBOLIC. It does not have causes, but only one cause. Howsoever different the suffering is, the cause is always one. The cause is that the hidden harmony between the human mind and the cosmic existence is lost. Whenever the hidden harmony is broken, suffering arises.

So suffering is only symbolic of broken harmony. In fact, even physiological suffering is symbolic of the harmony in the body being broken. Mental suffering is symbolic of the harmony in the mind being broken. Wherever harmony is broken, there is suffering.

Suffering really means broken harmony, and bliss means harmony regained. You can say it like this: harmony is bliss and the absence of harmony is suffering. So whenever and wherever there is not harmony in any dimension – physiological, mental or spiritual – you will have suffering.

The deeper the level, the more suffering there is. On a physiological level, when there is no harmony you have pain. It is not so deep. It can be removed by outward methods because it is superficial. It is only the first layer, the physiological. It can be helped to be thrown out. Medicines can help, chemicals can

SUFFERING: BROKEN HARMONY

help, and your health can be regained.

This word *health* must be understood, because health really means harmony. The word *health* comes from the same root from which *whole* and *holy* come. The moment the body is whole, it is healthy. When the body is broken into parts, it is diseased. The word *disease* is also to be noted. It means dis-eased: two parts not at ease. But on the physiological level, outward help is easily possible because physiology is your outer part, your outermost part.

When it is the psyche, the mind, and if the mind's harmony is broken, then you have not pain, but anguish. Then the suffering is deeper, and at the most outward help can make you adjusted, not harmonious. On the physiological level, outward help can make you harmonious, healthy, whole, but the mind can be helped only up to the limit of adjustment.

So the whole of Western psychology is doing nothing but creating adjustments. Freud said somewhere that the most that we can hope for through psychology and psychoanalysis is normal insanity. We can only hope for normal insanity. In his last years, he writes to some friends: "I cannot hope for happiness for the human mind. At the most, we can make him adjusted to normal unhappiness."

Any outward help cannot go very deep as far as the mind is concerned. It can only make you adjusted. And the word *adjusted* really means nothing because with each culture, adjustment is different. A person who is well-adjusted in an Eastern society is not so adjusted in a Western society. In a particular religion, one may be adjusted, in another religion, he may become maladjusted. So adjustment is a criterion which is more sociological than psychological. It is concerned more with the society to which you are adjusted.

When the innermost part of you – the inner being, the spiritual – is not in harmony, then not even adjustment from without can help. And something more can be understood. The innermost, the central part of your being is not reached at all through psychoanalysis, through any science of the mind that is prevalent today. In fact, in Western languages you have nothing parallel with *pain* and *anguish* as far as the third, innermost part is concerned – no word. *Pain* is physiological, *anguish* is mental, but when the spirit, your being, is not in harmony, is unhealthy, then you have no word for it.

Buddha used the word *dukkha*. It cannot be translated really. It is neither pain nor anguish nor misery. *Dukkha* means an existence without meaning, a meaningless existence. You go on existing without any meaning, you go on existing unnecessarily, you become just a burden to yourself. That is what is meant by *dukkha*: you have become just a burden to yourself.

Buddha was not physically ill. He had one of the most beautiful and harmonious physiques. He was not in anguish. There was no psychological complexity, no psychological disharmony. He was one of the most adjusted beings, but he felt *dukkha*.

So I will have to explain to you what *dukkha* is. That is real suffering; *dukkha* is the innermost suffering.

The whole story will have to be told to you.

When Buddha was born, all the wise men came to bless him. One wise man came from the Himalayas. The moment he saw Siddhartha – Buddha's name – he began to weep. Buddha's father was disturbed. He asked, "Why are you weeping? You have come to bless the child and instead you are weeping. Is something going to be wrong with the child?"

The wise old man said, "No, nothing is going to be wrong with the child. I am weeping for myself. This child is going to be a buddha, an enlightened one, and I will not be there. I am going to die this year; my course is completed. And I have been seeking and searching for a man who is enlightened, but I couldn't find one in my life. This child is going to be an enlightened one, but I will not be there. That's why I am weeping."

But this forecast disturbed the father even more, because if Buddha, if Siddhartha, is going to be enlightened, then what will become of his kingdom?

He asked the other wise men how to stop the child. They said, "There are only two possibilities. If he can be prevented from becoming aware of suffering, of *dukkha*, only then can you hold him, otherwise he is going to be a sannyasin. So don't let him know suffering, don't let him know *dukkha*."

The father could not understand how they could prevent someone from knowing *dukkha*. So he again asked for advice.

They advised him that Siddhartha should not see death, otherwise life would become meaningless. He should not become aware of death; he should not know at all that death exists, that life is going to end. He should not become aware that old age comes; otherwise, youth will become meaningless. And he should *never* see a sannyasin, he should never see a sannyasin, otherwise if he sees a dancing, laughing, blissful sannyasin, his life will again become meaningless. So these three conditions were to be fulfilled: he should not see a diseased old man, he shouldn't see someone who is dead, and he shouldn't see someone blissful.

Siddhartha's father arranged things in such a way that not even a dead leaf was seen by him, and no old man came nearby. Whenever he passed through the streets, the whole street would be arranged in such a way that no old man passed by. He was not aware that there is death and he was never allowed to see any sannyasin.

But how long can you prevent this? One day there was going to be a youth festival. Siddhartha was invited to preside over it. Young men and young women had come from all over the kingdom. He was riding on his chariot and some old man passed by. He asked his driver, "What has happened to this man?"

The chariot driver said, "I cannot deceive you. Nothing has happened to this man. This happens to everybody."

Siddharth asked him, "Will I also be like that some day?"

The chariot driver said, "I cannot deceive you. No one is an exception."

THE ETERNAL QUEST

So Siddharth said, "Then let us go back. It is no use going to the youth festival. I have become an old man. If old age is to come, it has come anyway, and youth is useless because it is just a hiding place for old age."

When they were driving back, a dead body was being carried by. Siddharth asked, "What has happened?"

The chariot driver said, "The second stage: after old age, this happens."

Buddha says, "Then I am dead! Then life makes no sense at all. It is meaningless, it is futile."

Then back home, just when he was at the door to his palace, he saw a sannyasin.

The parable tells it like this: that all this was impossible, that all this couldn't just happen, so this dead man, this old man, and the sannyasin were arranged by destiny, by the deities – this couldn't just happen. The tale, the myth, went like this: that this was all arranged by the deities because otherwise Buddha will not feel suffering. And if suffering is not felt, then you cannot attain that inner harmony which is bliss.

Dukkha means the knowledge that whatsoever appears to be living is going to die, whatsoever appears to be blissful is not so. And as we live, ordinary life is going to end in death; it is just a progression toward death. So on the third level, the innermost, suffering means *dukkha*; you can also say "spiritual agony." And I would like to tell you that today there are very few persons who are spiritually in agony, who are in *dukkha*.

The anguish is there, the mental agony is there, the mental disharmony is there – and in the West, it is intense. In the East it is not so intense; the mental agony is not so intense. And the reason? The reason is this, that mental agony becomes intense only when physical pain is not there. When physical pain is less, only then is your consciousness freed from the physiological level and can go to the mental.

And the same again happens when there is no mental agony

SUFFERING: BROKEN HARMONY

and the mental realm becomes harmonious: you become aware of spiritual suffering, spiritual agony. If the body is suffering – as it is suffering in the East – you will not feel mental agony. You have no energy left to feel it; you are exhausted by the day-to-day struggle to survive. The day-to-day struggle for the body to somehow survive exhausts you so much that on the mental level you are simply tired, not in anguish. So whenever a society becomes materially prosperous, mental agony is deepened, but whenever a society is poor, mental agony is not there.

This is not a good sign. In the East people think this is a good sign that we are in less mental agony than people in the West. But it is not a good sign at all. It simply shows that we are more poor, more hungry, more starved. We are so much engaged with the body that we cannot pay any attention to the mind. As far as the mind is concerned, we only feel tiredness, that's all.

So this is the difference: in the East, pain is predominant, physical pain is predominant, physical suffering, is predominant; in the West, psychic pain, mental agony, has become predominant. And this is a sign of progress; this is a sign of progress. The East must also come at least up to this level – of being mentally in anguish.

You have arranged the whole – there is no pain, there is no anguish – but then what? When there is pain you are struggling for something – for a house, for a body. You are struggling for it. There is something to do, and to be engaged in and occupied with. When the body is okay, then the mind suffers. It becomes aware of intrinsic contradictions, intrinsic tensions.

But if and when this happens, if you are also not in mental anguish, if there is harmony as far as the mind is concerned, then you become aware of a deeper meaninglessness. Then you become worried on a more fundamental dimension. The body is okay, the mind is okay – now you yourself are meaningless.

Meditation is to help the mind regain harmony. In fact, meditation leads you only up to the last boundary of the mind; no method can lead you to the spiritual. No method can lead you to the spiritual, it can only lead you to a mental harmony. And when mental harmony is attained you become aware of a deeper realm of yourself, because you need not be concerned at all with the mind now.

So the West doesn't only need psychoanalysis. That only gives a superficial adjustment. The West needs meditation. It needs methods of meditation that can give authentic psychic harmony. Then you become aware of a suffering, of *dukkha*, meaninglessness. But one has to be aware of this innermost suffering. This awareness is a great bliss in disguise, because once you become aware that life is meaningless – that death is awaiting you, that everything just ends and leads nowhere; that the whole of life, the whole effort, just leads to the grave, that you just end – then this suffering, this *dukkha* and the awareness of it, is the point from where you can take a jump into another realm, into another dimension.

It is not that you will find meaning in life – it is not so. It is not that there will be no death now – it is not so. But once the boundary of the mind is crossed, you become aware of this inner suffering, this meaninglessness. This feeling of meaninglessness is still bound with your past.

You could never conceive of existence as meaningless, you have always been purposeful. That's why this suffering comes to you. But once you take the jump... And you cannot go back; there is no way to go back. Once you have come to the end limit of the mind, you have come to a point of no return. You cannot go back, and before you there is meaninglessness and death. If you can stay in it, if you can be courageous enough to be in it, if you can be a witness to it, then there is an explosion. Then the suffering is lost.

Then there is no suffering, then there is no longing for meaning, then there is no desire for immortality. Then the seriousness has gone, then you become playful. Then everything changes into a new dimension – the dimension of play, the dimension of *leela*. Only then is the harmony between you and the cosmic,

SUFFERING: BROKEN HARMONY

between you and existence, regained within you. Then there is no barrier because then there is no mind.

The mind is a search for meaning; the mind is a search for immortality. Or you can say that the ego is in fear of death and if there is no meaning, then the ego has no foothold to stand upon. This gap is the spiritual abyss. From the mind, from the boundary of the mind, you will become aware of a spiritual agony, a meaninglessness, and death as the only goal. If you jump into it, into the abyss, then there is mutation, then there is no suffering, then you become blissful. And then there will never be any suffering at all, because the whole point of suffering is lost – the ego is lost, the mind is lost.

Now you can look at this in another way. The body becomes unhealthy if the body is in tension, disharmonious within itself or with the atmosphere. The mind becomes anguished if it is in conflict with itself or with other minds. Your being feels meaninglessness; because of your body and your mind you become alienated with the cosmic spirit. Because of your body and your mind – these two boundaries – you become alien, a stranger, uprooted from the cosmic existence. You feel suffering. If these two barriers are not there, you have become one. Then there is no question of meaning for you. You are not, the cosmic is. You don't need any goal. Now you cannot die because you are not, the cosmic is. Now you are just a wave in the ocean. Even if the wave disappears, it remains in the ocean, the ocean remains. Now you have come to realize yourself as the ocean so there is no fear of death. Death is not. As far as your cosmic being is concerned, death is not.

But as far as your individual being, your ego being, is concerned, death is. And all the meanings that we look for, search for, desire, are ego meanings: "I must attain something otherwise I am no one. I can only feel fulfilled if I achieve something." Only through achievement is the ego fulfilled, otherwise, "I am no one, so I must achieve something – maybe riches, maybe prestige, maybe knowledge. I must attain something, I must attach something to me which I can claim as mine, my achievement. Only then there is 'I'; otherwise I am no one."

The mind feels anguish, and the mind feels suffering, *dukkha*. The mind feels anguish as far as mental disharmony is concerned, and the mind feels suffering, *dukkha*, as far as ultimate suffering is concerned – but this feeling is of the mind. So you must know this distinction clearly. Mind is in anguish as far as mental inner disharmony is concerned; mind is in *dukkha*, suffering, as far as the ego meaning and the ultimate destiny are concerned.

Once the mind is not, the mind is annihilated, there is no suffering at all, no *dukkha* at all. Body pain is possible even for an enlightened one. Even for a buddha, body pain is possible, but no psychic anguish is possible, and no *dukkha* is possible.

Suffering has these three dimensions. To me, the ultimate suffering is because of the ego, and the ultimate bliss comes only through egolessness.

The Western mind has become more anguished because of scientific achievement. The ego is strengthened more, and when the ego is strengthened…

This is because science took an attitude of conquering nature. Conquering nature is a very egoistic attitude, and because for these last three centuries we have had a constant conditioning of everybody through science, the mind is science oriented, especially in the West. It thinks in terms of conquering nature, it thinks in terms of competing with others.

And the more science has progressed, the more the Western mind has felt that religion is invalid, because so many propositions by religion have been proved wrong by scientific evolution. But really, no religious statement can be proved wrong by any scientific progress. Only those scientific statements of older days, of ancient days, which were recorded in the religious scriptures have been found to be invalid. They are not religious statements at all. If in the Bible, the earth is said to be flat, it is not a religious statement. Religion is at all not concerned with whether

SUFFERING: BROKEN HARMONY

the earth is flat or not. This is a scientific statement from the days of Jesus which has been proved invalid. It only shows that the older science has been proved invalid by the newer science, but not that religion has at all.

And this misfortune happens and has deeper consequences because in the old days, the religious scriptures were the only record. In fact, Bible means "the book." It was the only book in those days. It is an encyclopedia. It has no name really. It means "the book."

The Vedas have no name really. *Vedas* only means "the knowledge." All the knowledge of those days has been compiled: the Vedas have poetry, they have science, they have medicine, they have grammar, they have religion, they have philosophy. The Vedas have everything; they are encyclopedias.

But because the scientific knowledge of those days is compiled in them, and newer science, newer researches, disproves it, it doesn't mean that religion is disproved. Not a single religious statement can be disproved by science because the dimensions are altogether different. They never crisscross, they cross nowhere at all. Whatsoever Einstein says, never crosses Jesus anywhere, just as no progress in mathematics, in higher mathematics, can prove Kalidas or Shakespeare wrong. This is because it has no relevance: poetry has its own dimension, mathematics has its own dimension. And however great a poet is, he cannot refute any mathematical statement with his poetry – howsoever deep it is. It makes no sense.

So scientific progress has given a false attitude to the Western mind: that religion is refuted. And if religion is refuted, if there is no divine, no divineness, if there is no cosmic relationship possible, then you are left alone, uprooted. That's why this century is the century of alienation in the West. Everyone feels alienated. And the further scientific progress goes, the more you will feel a stranger in a world in which you have no roots.

If we go back, if we ask some Vedic *rishi*, he will say he lives in a cosmic family. Everything is related; even the sun is related, the stars are related, the moon is related. They are persons; it is a great family. He is rooted in it. He is related intimately with everything that exists. He is not alone. There is a cosmic relationship running with each breath.

But today, the educated mind is absolutely uprooted – no relationship at all. The cosmic family has disappeared. The stars are dead, you cannot be related to them. Existence is material, no relationship can exist, and everything is inimical to you. That is bound to come; that is the conclusion, the logical conclusion. Either you will be rooted in existence, or the whole of existence will become inimical to you. These are the only two alternatives; you cannot remain neutral.

Scientific progress denied any relationship with the universe. But those deniers never have thought that now the second step will have to be taken, in which the whole becomes inimical to the individual. That is the Western anguish today: no relationship. The family has disappeared, the cosmic family.

And now the smaller family will have to disappear – it is disappearing. If I am not related to the earth, how can I be related to the mother? The logic is the same. The older *rishi* will call the earth "mother." He will go on calling the earth, "Mother Earth." He will call existence, "father" – "Father Sky." We deny it. We never thought that this denial will have a logical conclusion in the end. If we deny the cosmic family, then the smaller unit of the family will be denied altogether.

If I am not related with the earth, if I am not related with the sky, if I am not related with existence itself, then what difference does it make how I am related to my mother, to my father? If I am not related to nature – and my mother and my father are just parts of nature to me – if I am not related to the cosmic existence and they are just parts of the cosmic existence, then I am not related to them. Then I become one, alone, and there is darkness everywhere – because only a loving relationship creates light, otherwise there is darkness; only love is light, otherwise there is darkness. So everywhere is darkness, and everywhere is the enemy. Friendship is inconceivable; I have just to struggle and fight – but for what? The anguish comes. I am alone.

And if you are not related, and you think there is no possibility of any relationship, then you will never transcend your psychic realm, you will never come to the spiritual, because you can come to it only when you are related to the cosmic, otherwise you never will. Our personality is a flowering amidst relationships. The deeper you go into relationships, the truer it will look.

If a child is broken away from his mother, he will not be the same person as he would have been with his mother, because something grows in a relationship that will not grow now; the child will be retarded. We have roots, just like trees – invisible, of course. The child has roots with his mother.

They have experimented in many ways; they have done so many experiments with so many animals. The mother is denied. From the very first day the mother is absent, the animal grows alone. He never grows really. Everything is provided – better than his mother can provide – everything is provided. Only the mother's love is absent. He never grows. He becomes insane, he becomes perverted. And in the end, he is never found to be capable of love. He cannot love because the roots of love have been broken. With the mother, it is not only that she is caring for the child. Unknown even to herself, something is flowing from her toward the child.

And it is not only that the mother is giving something. The child is always giving responses. So whenever a child is born, it is not only that a child is born. On that very day, the mother is also born; otherwise she was just a woman. And there is a vast difference between a woman and a mother: something new has come to her, something new has flowered in her. So the child is giving something. It is reciprocal, it is mutual. The mother grows into motherhood. She becomes a different personality altogether.

I have just taken this as an example.

A child growing in a family, in a great family, has a different personality when grown. A child growing in an individual family has a different personality. The roots are less deep.

Religion means finding roots with the ultimate, finding roots with the cosmos. Even the sun should not be unrelated to you, even the river flowing by should not be unrelated to you, even the trees should not be unrelated to you, the earth should not be unrelated to you. Everything should be related to you as it is related to the all.

This relationship is religion. The word *religion* means *religere*, to be related to the whole, related from all sides, from everywhere. If you are related in this way to the whole, then there is no suffering, because then there is no possibility of death. You cannot die because *you* are not, the whole is. And the whole has always been and the whole will always be. Then you are not in fear. You will always be – even if a drop, you will be in the ocean, lost, but you will be. Then there is no fear of death, then there is no problem of meaning. Then you are not alone, then you are not in struggle, in conflict.

Another thing to be understood: science has taken a very inimical attitude toward nature; religion takes a very friendly attitude. It is not that we are to fight with nature, it is that we are to understand it. And it would be a great transformation for science if science could take this attitude – not of fighting, but of understanding. Fighting creates hatred all around. It exists only in hatred.

Understanding can exist only in a love relationship. Religion thinks in terms of understanding the whole. And the more you understand it, the more you are in it. Then you are not outside, then you are not an outsider; then you are in.

This feeling of is-ness is ecstatic. If you can feel "in" in the whole – an innermost part of it – then you are at ease. Then you can never be dis-eased, Then you are at ease. Greater are the hands you are in, greater are the forces you can rely upon. You are not unnecessarily burdened; you are not alone. You do not have to carry the whole burden on your head. You are just like a child sleeping in his mother's lap, unburdened, carefree. The mother is

SUFFERING: BROKEN HARMONY

there, so he need not care. There is no anguish, no suffering.

Religion has this attitude toward the whole. The cosmic is just like the mother. Your are in it, with greater forces, infinite forces, with wisdom you cannot fathom. Then you are at ease. This at-easeness, this let-go, is a situation in which there is a flowering, an innocent, unburdened flowering.

To me, this flowering is *anand* – bliss, ecstasy. *Dukkha*, suffering, is a retarded flowering which couldn't flower into the whole, which remained aloof, which uprooted itself from the whole, from the earth. It will have suffering. It is bound to happen. It will have suffering and only death, and no life really.

Western science has given a conditioning which has made man egoistic, alone. The Eastern concept of knowledge, knowing, is very different. It is "in cooperation with." It is not that we are to force nature to reveal its mysteries. On the contrary, it is to open ourselves in a loving participation with nature so that nature reveals its mysteries: it is just asking the mother, just questioning the mother; you are not to force her.

So science has come upon so many understandings, but they have been forcibly taken. They have blood marks, they have been violent. And any discovery that is violent, any knowledge that is violent, is going to end in greater violence. Nature will take its revenge. We are just nonentities, and we have been fighting with the cosmic existence, the cosmic force. We can be put off in just a minute, in just a single second.

But man thinks himself the master. This nonsense of being the master has created the whole chaos. This ego masquerading as the master has created the whole chaos. The Western mind will go deeper and deeper into anguish unless this absolutely false attitude – not only false, this harmful attitude of science – is thrown out altogether.

Nature cannot be forced, should not be forced. I will tell you something: even Eastern minds have come to know many things from nature through different methods, altogether different methods. If you go to old Iranian or Indian medicine books, it is a miracle, because no laboratories existed and there are *lakhs* and *lakhs* of medicines without laboratory methods, and a single person writing about thousands and thousands of medicines – a single person. A single discovery would have been enough, but there is one person writing about thousands and thousands of things. And even today, when there are laboratory methods, the old findings are not denied. But the old medicine books say that these were not findings made in laboratories, these were findings made through meditation. Now, we cannot believe it. It is said that Lukman will go, sit under a tree, meditate, and ask the tree, in meditation, "For what can you be used?" He will sit in meditation under the tree and when he is deep in trance – when the mind is not there, he is empty, vacant, receptive – he will just pray to the tree, "Tell me for what use your leaves can be." And the tree will answer, and he will just note down.

This seems unbelievable. How can this be possible? But if it is not possible, then the other possibility is even more impossible, because Lukman had no laboratories. No method of chemical analysis existed. Even today, Lukman is not refuted. Any experimentation proves him right again.

You know serpentina, a sleep-creating chemical. It has been known in India for ten thousand years as *serpgandha*. The newer name is just a translation of *serpgandha*: serpentina. And all the qualities of *serpgandha* that have been written about in ancient Indian books have found to be exactly so, through all the chemical research. But there is no method given, they didn't know any, so how did they come to know all the qualities of the drug?

As far as they are concerned, they say it was through meditation, asking the serpgandha itself. And as I have worked deeply upon meditation, and as I have worked through so many channels upon meditation, I can be a witness that this is a possibility. But this is a possibility of a very different approach: through participation with nature – not fighting, through participating.

But this is something to be noted, that all the scientific

SUFFERING: BROKEN HARMONY

inventions began in the East. Scientific thinking has become prevalent in the West for only the last three hundred years. All the inventions, the beginnings, were in the East, but they never developed. Why? If the beginnings were there, and there was every opportunity to proceed from those beginnings into completion, then why?

In China, ammunition was known three thousand years ago. They just played with it, just fire play, they never used it for war. They knew everything about it, but they never used it. Why? If you ask them – if you ask Taoist thinkers – they will say, "If you participate with nature, if you ask nature itself, then nature will itself prohibit you: 'Don't go further than this. Don't go any further!'" It looks like the West needs that advice, "Don't go any further." But the Western mind seems obsessed with progress, as if progress in itself is something meaningful. If you have created the atom bomb then you are obsessed with creating the hydrogen bomb. The atom bomb is enough, more than enough, but the mind is obsessed. And the whole thing can end in chaos, it is ending in chaos. It is coming to the end, because we have been fighting, we have never asked nature itself where to stop.

Knowledge is not always a good. It can prove a great evil. It is only good up to the limit where it can be managed. But now we have transgressed that limit. It is not that we are managing knowledge. On the contrary, the knowledge is managing and controlling us. It seems that we cannot do anything else: we have to take another step, knowing very well that another step may prove fatal. And there is no one to prevent us, because we are our own advisers, with no advice from the beyond – as if children have become the master of the house, with no elder to give them advice.

Even if the elder is there, he is locked away. The suffering has become deep, intense, because of us. And we have not been able to transform the suffering which can be transformed into bliss, because all the doors are closed. We ourselves have closed them.

THE ETERNAL QUEST

"There is no God." Then we have closed the door; there is not even the possibility. It is not even scientific to say that there is no God. This much can be said scientifically: that science has not yet found any God. Then there is still a possibility.

But we say that there is no God. The possibility is closed. And once the possibility is closed, once the suggestion has been taken that there is no God, your mind will not look in that direction again. It will look everywhere, but not in that direction. It is closed. And that is the only possibility of transcending suffering.

Nietzsche said a hundred years before that God is dead – a very prophetic saying because the days that followed proved this: that as far as we are concerned, this twentieth century is concerned, God is dead for us. Not that God *is* dead, but that we are so closed in ourselves that for us there is no God. But it makes no difference to God. If there is no God, it makes a great difference to us, because a great possibility, a great relationship, is closed. We are thrown upon ourselves. Now we cannot go anywhere, now we cannot transcend the human mind. Because there is no possibility, not even a hypothetical possibility has been left, where can you go?

You can, at the most, go back to the animals and nowhere else. There is no beyond, there is only the below. And if the beyond is dropped, then you will fall below. This is one of the fundamental laws of nature: either you go further or you will be pushed behind. You cannot stand still; there is no situation which is a standstill situation.

In his autobiography, Eddington says somewhere that the word *rest* is meaningless. There is no rest to be found anywhere: everything is either going ahead or going back. You cannot be at rest. So if you deny the beyond, then there is nowhere further to go, and you cannot remain yourself because the suffering is so much, the anguish is so much. To be human is to be so anguished, so tense, that you cannot feel it, so you have to fall back. So you use some intoxicant, and you fall back; you are mad after sex and you fall back. You go back somewhere to the animals.

SUFFERING: BROKEN HARMONY

But you cannot go back. You can only try, because no going back is really possible. You can just try. It is just like jumping in the sky. By jumping, you cannot go there, you come back again. For a moment you feel that you are in the sky, but then the earth again attracts you; you gravitate again to the earth. By jumping, you cannot go to the moon, but you can jump toward it. For a single moment there is an illusion that you are now out of gravitation, out of gravity, but before you know it you have to come back. So you can just go in jumps toward the animals, but you fall back upon being human, and to be human has become such an anguish. It always was, but there was a possibility to transcend. Now there is no possibility. That's why the anguish is more intense, frustrating. And it cannot be used as a means.

The whole art of religion is concerned with how to transform darkness into light, how to transform death into deathlessness, how to transform your suffering into bliss. The whole art, the whole alchemy of religion, is concerned with this.

Buddha was also in suffering, Mahavira was also in suffering, Christ was also in suffering, but they could transform their suffering into a deep bliss. We cannot transform it. What has happened? The possibility is denied.

To me, your suffering shows the possibility. You cannot suffer unless there is a possibility of transcending. A person who cannot be healthy cannot feel illness. It is impossible. If you feel illness, it shows there is a possibility that you can be helped; otherwise you cannot feel it. Only the capacity for being healthy can feel the actuality of illness. If you feel darkness, that shows you can know light. A blind man cannot even feel darkness because to see darkness you need eyes. You cannot see without eyes. Darkness is an eye phenomenon, as much as light. We ordinarily think then those who are blind will be living in darkness, total darkness. This is completely absurd. A blind man cannot know darkness. Darkness is an eye perception. So if you can feel darkness all around, you are capable of knowing light. The eye is there, and the eye which is capable of knowing light, knows darkness, otherwise it cannot know.

So when I say that the suffering is there, I mean that the suffering shows that bliss is possible. If there is no possibility of bliss, then you cannot feel suffering. You feel it because of the absence. This is the absence which is felt as suffering.

So the possibility has to be opened up again, and the gates have to be made wider than they were before. Even as they were before, they have to be made wider, because the present-day mind will need wider gates, wider openings, otherwise they will go on denying. The cosmic must burst forth upon us. Everyone can become a gate. If you can transcend your suffering, you will become a gate, and through you, many will know that something beyond exists.

This is the work to be done. Go, wander on the whole earth. But first become a gate so that whosoever may come in contact with you knows that there is something beyond, that something exists beyond.

That is the only hope. If we can make it felt that the beyond exists through our eyes, through our very being; if we can make it felt that the beyond exists, that bliss exists, then, only then, can this humanity be saved. Otherwise, that which is going to happen – if nothing interferes – is not hopeful.

The East is going to turn materialist. The East is going to turn materialist because it is so starved. It is bound to go on the same lines, on the same technological and scientific lines, as the West has gone. It will follow the West. So if a Buddha comes today in the East, he will really not be welcome. The East can welcome Einstein but not Buddha. The East is becoming materialist day by day.

The East will become communist, materialist. And the West: if something intervenes, if some openings are there, if some people become so concerned with meditation that it becomes a life and death matter with them; if they transcend their suffering and become openings to the divine, then the West can turn to a spiritual age. Otherwise the West is going not materialist but

SUFFERING: BROKEN HARMONY

mad. It will go mad because it has come to the end limit of mind, and now there is no beyond. The beyond is denied. It has become a taboo to talk of the divine, to talk of the spiritual. It is taboo. You feel not to talk about it, people may think you crazy.

So day by day the West is going mad, insane. And in insanity, much, much will happen there. LSD will come, mescaline will come, marijuana will be there. These are only escapades, escapes – escapes from the overcoming madness which is just around the corner. You know it is coming. You can only escape into oblivion. You just take some drug; be unconscious. Then you don't care. But your not caring will not prevent it. It is coming, and if you are unconscious, it will come sooner.

These are the possibilities. If there is no intervention, if nothing intervenes, then these are the possibilities. The East will turn materialist and West is going neurotic. Both are not good. And the East cannot remain non-neurotic for much longer because it is only a matter of time, within a century, that the same will happen in the East. After materialism, after a violent science, after a God-denying culture, there is no possibility. There is no open space, there is nowhere to go.

But something can intervene. So I am not a pessimist. Something can intervene. But I cannot go on just hoping for it, that something may intervene. We have to become vehicles for that intervention to come. Each one has to become a passage for the divine to come to the earth.

This is what *my* sannyas means. I will try to make you a vessel, a vehicle, a window, a door through which the beyond can peek. Just a ray, even, will be a great phenomenon. If you can be witnesses…

This is the first time upon earth that no one is really a witness. Everyone goes on quoting others. If you ask some atheist, he is just himself. He will say, "There is no God" but if you ask some theist, he will say, "Yes, there is God. My father says so," or "my father's father" or "some ancient *rishi* has said so." For the divine there is no witness who can say, "I say so," who can

THE ETERNAL QUEST

say, "I am the witness" – who not only can say it, but can live the witness; his being can become a witness.

God, the God dimension, the divine dimension, has lost its hold because so many neurotic people, so many diseased people, became interested in religion. They always become interested, they always do, because all those who are frustrated become interested. They take their frustration as their interest with the divine. Their interest is negative. They are diseased within, so when they become interested in the divine, they become the wrong kind of witnesses. They are not blissful, they are not happy. They are sad images of sorrow. They close the gate rather than opening it.

This gate of the divine can be open only if those who are concerned with it become so blissful, so happy, so dancing… Only a dancing God can replace Nietzsche's verdict that God is dead, only a dancing God can contradict Nietzsche's statement that God is dead, because only a dancing God can prove that godliness is living.

So be a witness to it. Don't think of others' suffering. Transcend your suffering and then you will be a help to others. Don't think of serving others. Serve yourself first, transcend your suffering. Then you will be a servant to all, and you do something which means something, which is significant. Don't be a sad servant. Don't make it a duty. That will just strengthen your ego. Servants have great egos, and they create so much mischief in the world. "Servants of the people" – they are the most mischievous element.

Become a door yourself. Transcend your suffering, mutate it. And don't take religion seriously. It has done very fatal harm. Be playful. Saints of the future must not be old shadow images, images of sorrow. Be blissful, laughing, playful – only then can the door be opened.

If you can create a magnetic atmosphere of bliss around you, only then can you ttract those who have fallen victims of atheism, who have fallen victims of so much nonsensical, but so-called scientific, philosophy. Transcend yourself, and you will transcend it. First be aware of it, then live with it. Don't escape. If there is suffering, live with it.

And this is a miracle law, that if you can live with any suffering you will transcend it. Don't escape, don't run, don't hide. Face it, encounter it, live with it. It is there. Take it as a fact, live with it. It is difficult, it is going to be arduous, but when you come to transcend it, then you know that you have found it without paying anything. It seems arduous in the process, but in the end, when there is the realization of the bliss, you have not paid anything at all.

Don't think of others' suffering. Transcend yours and use it. It is a great energy. When you get it, it will become bliss. Then take life as a play. Take life as a play; go on playing it. Only in a play you can be egoless. Only in a play you are not. You can be absent, you are not needed.

When you are absent, only then you become related to the cosmic. And to be related with the cosmic is the only ecstasy.

Enough for today.

15

The Last Luxury

Osho,
On every other street corner in India, it seems one sees beggars who claim to be sadhus, renunciates. Are they just parasites and exploiters, or are they really authentic holy men?

EVERYTHING THAT CAN ALSO BE HELPFUL can be harmful. For every authentic coin, there is a false coin that can be interpreted as authentic. But it cannot be avoided. If it is understood then the likelihood can be lessened, but it can never be absolutely avoided. The only way to avoid it is to throw away the authentic coin also. If the authentic is to exist, the false will follow inevitably because it is easier to be false, it is not so arduous.

To really be a sadhu is the most arduous adventure possible. It is the greatest demand and challenge to the human mind. But to be one of the so-called sadhus that you see all over India is not a demand, not a challenge. Once a country has seen people like Krishna, Buddha, and Mahavira, the image is exploited. To me, the exploitation shows that the authentic has existed. The false coin only shows that there has been an authentic coin. The false is accepted because people have known the authentic – the false can masquerade as the authentic. But the moment the authentic is lost, the false will disappear as well. Then you cannot be exploited.

If there was no such thing as an authentic sadhu, then the falsehood could not continue to exist. But one of the contradictions of life is that everything exists in opposition, in relation, to something else. Even a false sadhu has appeared because the masses have known the authentic and the longing for the authentic lingers.

Osho,
Then how can one tell if a sadhu is authentic or not?

There is no need. If someone becomes a sadhu, it is his own private affair. There is no need to pay any attention to him. Whether he is fake or authentic is his affair. His belief is a private affair, his being a sadhu is a private thing. Once it becomes public there will always be fakes, there will always be false people who will exploit. If someone is a poet it is his own affair, if someone is a dancer it is his own affair, if someone is a sadhu it is his own affair. He should not be worshipped – not even if he is authentic. If the authentic is worshipped, then the false will follow automatically and there will be those who exploit the phenomenon.

The need to recognize who is an authentic sadhu arises only when you want to worship someone. If you want to worship, then you have to know whether the person is authentic or false. But if you are not going to worship, there is no need to question whether the person is authentic. He may be, he may not be. It is his affair.

Unless and until we learn that to be a sadhu is one's own affair – no one else need be concerned with it – the false cannot be stopped from exploiting. And because of the false, the authentic is lost. The moment there is no worship, the moment there is no special respect given to the sadhu, only the authentic will remain.

Only through respect and worshipping can the false exploit. To the false, being a sadhu is not the attraction. The attraction comes from the worshipper. No one should be worshipped. Sadhus must not be treated with any special awe. Once they are not given any special attention, the false will disappear and only the authentic will remain.

An authentic sadhu is one for whom the world has become unreal, for whom another dimension has come into existence, for whom this maya is not the reality. This is not a belief; it is his experience. The whole existence has become divine. That is what the person has experienced; it has been an existential experience. To me, this is a sadhu.

No outward criteria will be applicable because an authentic person will never be an imitation. He will not be an imitation buddha, he will be himself. So it is not important what he wears, what he eats, how he behaves. All that will come spontaneously to him. Only the false can imitate, never the authentic. The authentic is always individual, so there can be no models and no predecessors.

This is also to be noted; that only a false sadhu will behave like a sadhu. The authentic one will behave like himself. That's why, when a Jesus appears, he seems like an upstart.

Upstarts never seem like upstarts because they follow a fixed pattern. But an authentic man appears to be an upstart because he is not following the traditional pattern of other sadhus. He is himself.

So you will always think that the authentic man has gone wrong, he has gone to the devil, while the false man goes on being worshipped because he can imitate. It is not difficult; every type of criteria can be imitated. Then the personality becomes double: when the public is watching he is one person, he imitates the outward manifestations of a religious man, and when he is alone, he is someone else. There is a division: a public face and a private face.

But as far as a real sadhu is concerned, he has no private self and no public selves. He is one. That becomes his difficulty. Whatsoever he is, he always is. He is bound to be anti-traditional, bound to be a nonconformist.

So the irony is that the false will be worshipped and the real will be condemned.

THE LAST LUXURY

Osho,
Why are Westerners becoming so interested in Indian religions?

There is a deep reason. Religion is the last luxury so only an affluent society can afford religion. Religion is the flowering. When every so-called natural need is fulfilled, only then does the beyond become meaningful and significant. When body needs are fulfilled, when you are not in any struggle at the physical level, then a new struggle begins on a higher level. That is the struggle to achieve consciousness. So whenever a society becomes rich, only then does religion become meaningful. A poor society can never be religious.

Osho,
Isn't India religious?

Yes, India is religious. But India became religious when India was a rich country. Now it is just a hangover.

India was a rich country at the time of Buddha. It was at a peak, just like America is today. Patliputra was the same as New York is today. In the time of Buddha, India was at its golden peak. It could think in dimensions that are not confined to the body, not confined to the physical, visible world. So India could probe deeply into the ultimate mystery.

It is a strange fact that whenever a country becomes rich it becomes religious, and whenever a country becomes religious it is bound to fall back from its riches. When a country becomes religious it becomes otherworldly; this world becomes meaningless.

Osho,
Is it a vicious circle?

I won't say "vicious," I will just say "circle." You have to look at many things. To become young, you will have to become old; if you want to be born, you will have to die. If you consider death bad, then do not be born at all. If you consider old age bad, then do not be young at all – because to be young means that you are now on the way to being old. Life moves in circles. Nothing is bad.

A rich youth leads to a rich old age and a rich birth leads to a rich death. Religion is a flowering. Whenever a society reaches a point of leisure, art, meditation, religion flowers. Religion is the last flowering. But every flower is a sign that now the tree will die.

> Osho,
> Can religion or meditation help one to be more economically well off?
> Can it make a poor country rich?

No, it cannot. It is not an economic movement; it is a religious movement. It has a specific dimension within which to work. It can help a person to become more conscious, it can help a person to be more silent, it can help a person to be calm and collected, but it cannot help economically in any way.

If you take life as a whole, then to waste life only in economics and politics is a great wastage. If you take life as a whole, then ultimately whatsoever you achieve, the only achievement is what is inside you. All else is just superficial.

Religion and meditation cannot help to make a poor country rich in any way. It cannot. But it can help a poor man to be rich – in a very non-economic sense. If riches only mean the outward thing, then religion is absolutely irrelevant, but if you think in terms of inner consciousness, peace, a blissful attitude, a life lived as an inner celebration, then it can help. And to me, that is more meaningful.

THE LAST LUXURY

Osho,
What are your ideas on socialism?

Socialism to me is a very non-psychological way of thinking.

There is a longing to be equal, but that longing only shows that human beings are not equal in any dimension. They are unequal; the inequality is a fact. The concept of equality is only a fiction and whenever society hankers after a fiction, it falls into a chaotic way of life.

So socialism is not possible. It is an impossibility. It can only be possible if two conditions are present. The first is if the human mind is destroyed and man becomes a human automaton instead. Then socialism becomes possible because machines can be equal.

And socialists will go on trying to do this. They have been trying to wipe out the mind. Freedom of the mind will be the first target for socialism to clear away because freedom of the mind basically creates inequality.

Osho,
What about socialism not as a means of creating equality but only as a means of providing everyone with the basic necessities of life?

This vision of providing the basic necessities of life cannot be fulfilled, because one of the basic necessities is to be unequal. It is one of the very basic necessities. To be unequal to be oneself, to not be just a number but a name – not even a name, but a signature. That is one of the basic necessities, more basic than food, Food seems to be basic because the world is poor, but the moment everyone is fed it will cease to be a basic necessity; it will be forgotten. Clothes are not a basic necessity. They only seem to be because the world is naked. The moment plenty of clothes are available, it will not be a necessity.

Ultimately, mind is the only basic necessity. And it can never be fulfilled. The stomach can be fulfilled, naked bodies can be clothed and sheltered, and science has come to a point where socialism is not needed in order to provide these things They can be provided more easily without socialism. For example, Sweden has fulfilled the basic needs of its people better than Soviet Russia. These basic needs must be fulfilled but that doesn't require socialism. Socialism has not fulfilled these needs, rather, it has equalized poverty.

A poor man can be at ease with his poverty if everyone else is also very poor. Socialism has only equalized poverty. Even today, Soviet Russia is not a wealthy land. The poor in America are better off than the more successful people in Soviet Russia. But the poor person in America is not at ease because the comparison is there: others are rich.

Sudras were never as unhappy as they are now because everyone else in their world, in their class, was equally as poor. The world was taken for granted as being the way it was. It looked like a natural phenomenon, nothing could be done about it; it was determined by birth. It was taken for granted that to be a sudra was one's destiny. Competition was only possible between one sudra and another. But they were equally poor so they were at ease. The equal poverty was their consolation.

Now, when we have come to understand that a sudra is not born but made, the competition has moved from horizontal to vertical lines. The competition was very gentle between one sudra and another. Now the competition has become vertical. Everyone is competing with everyone else.

A capitalist society is a vertical society; a socialist society is a horizontal society. If you create a horizontal society, then the poverty will be evenly distributed. It is a consolation that everyone else is equally as poor, but the society will remain stagnant.

A socialist society is stagnant. That's why in the last five or ten years Soviet Russia has been moving away from socialism. That has been the basic controversy between Mao and Soviet Russia.

THE LAST LUXURY

Soviet Russia seems to Mao to be turning capitalistic now. It is no fault of Russia; it is because of a basic error in socialism itself. If socialism is to remain, it must become stagnant. The very inequality of individuals creates a restlessness to develop, to grow, to transcend. If everyone is equally placed, the society becomes stagnant. Then there is no motivation, there is no stimulation to work, to grow, to transcend. The motivation comes through inequality.

By and by, Soviet Russia will become capitalistic. It will have to. Otherwise it will die from stagnation. To me, a capitalist society is a natural phenomenon. A socialist structure is not natural. It is something imposed, something conceived of through the mind. Capitalism developed by itself; socialism has to be brought about, it cannot come by itself.

Marx thought it would happen, but he was basically wrong. And he has been proved to be wrong. He thought that socialism would be a natural outgrowth of capitalism – the more capitalistic a country is, the more possibility there is of a socialist revolution – but it has not happened that way

What has happened has been quite the contrary.

The less successful capitalist countries and the undeveloped countries, the poor countries that have no capitalism at all, have become more and more socialistic, while America has not become socialistic. According to Marx, socialism is a natural outgrowth of capitalism so America should be the first socialist country. It has not been so.

Socialism exploits the jealousy of the poor. To me, it is the greatest exploitation that has happened on earth. Capitalism has exploited the labor of the poor and socialism has exploited their souls. It is through jealousy that socialism steps in. But through jealousy, no revelation, no transformation can be achieved. It can kill, it can destroy, but it cannot create.

Socialism is a fiction. It is not scientific. To me, only a capitalist society is a scientific society. I am not saying that capitalism will remain as it is. It will go on growing and changing and all

THE ETERNAL QUEST

that socialism promises to fulfill will be fulfilled naturally. When affluence is created – and capitalism creates it – all the basic needs of survival will be there.

Soviet Russia has become successful not because it is a socialist society but because it has become a technological society. Poverty does not exist because of exploitation; it is because of the absence of a technology that is capable of fulfilling the needs of increasing numbers of people. Even if there is no exploitation, poverty will be there. In a primitive society, people are poor – more poor than they are now.

Real change will come about only through technology. The more technology progresses, the less human labor will be needed. And the moment human labor becomes superfluous, the whole structure of society will have to change.

A scientific, technological society will not be a socialist society. Capitalism creates competition and through competition, technology develops. If there is no competition then there will be no possibility of any growth. New techniques, new methodologies, are invented only through competition.

Russia has not invented anything new as far as their inner economy is concerned. Everything new that they have invented has been because of competition with America. Through competition, new techniques are invented. Russia is capitalistic in relation to its competitor America, and socialistic as far as its own economy is concerned. As far as the world market is concerned it is capitalistic, competitive. It is not socialistic – there are double standards.

But capitalism itself is not going to remain the way it is. It is going through a second revolution. The first revolution was industrial. the second will be technological.

ABOUT THE AUTHOR

OSHO DEFIES CATEGORIZATION, reflecting everything from the individual quest for meaning to the most urgent social and political issues facing society today. His books are not written but are transcribed from recordings of extemporaneous talks given over a period of thirty-five years. Osho has been described by *The Sunday Times* in London as one of the "1000 Makers of the 20th Century" and by *Sunday Mid-Day* in India as one of the ten people – along with Gandhi, Nehru and Buddha – who have changed the destiny of India.

Osho has a stated aim of helping to create the conditions for the birth of a new kind of human being, characterized as "Zorba the Buddha" – one whose feet are firmly on the ground, yet whose hands can touch the stars. Running like a thread through all aspects of Osho's talks and meditations is a vision that encompasses both the timeless wisdom of the East and the highest potential of Western science and technology.

He is synonymous with a revolutionary contribution to the science of inner transformation and an approach to meditation which specifically addresses the accelerated pace of contemporary life. The unique OSHO Active Meditations are designed to allow the release of accumulated stress in the body and mind so that it is easier to be still and experience the thought-free state of meditation.

OSHO INTERNATIONAL MEDITATION RESORT

EVERY YEAR the OSHO International Meditation Resort welcomes thousands of people from over 100 countries who come to enjoy and participate in its unique atmosphere of meditation and celebration. The 28-acre meditation resort is located in Pune, India, about 100 miles southeast of Mumbai (Bombay), in a tree-lined residential area set against a backdrop of bamboo groves and wild jasmine, peacocks and waterfalls.

The basic approach of the meditation resort is that of Zorba the Buddha: living in awareness, with a capacity to celebrate everything in life. Many visitors come to just be, to allow themselves the luxury of doing nothing. Others choose to participate in a wide variety of courses and sessions that support moving toward a more joyous and less stressful life by combining methods of self-understanding with awareness techniques. These courses are offered through OSHO Multiversity and take place in a pyramid complex next to the famous OSHO Teerth Park.

You can choose to practice various meditation methods, both active and passive, from a daily schedule that begins at six o'clock in the morning. Each evening there is a meditation event that moves from dance to silent sitting, using Osho's recorded talks as an opportunity to experience inner silence without effort.

Make online bookings for accommodation at the OSHO Guesthouse inside the meditation resort through the website below or drop us an email at guesthouse@osho.com

Take an online tour of the meditation resort, and access travel and program information at: www.osho.com/resort

The daily meditation schedule may include:

OSHO Dynamic Meditation: A technique designed to release tensions and repressed emotions, opening the way to a new vitality and an experience of profound silence.

OSHO Kundalini Meditation: A technique of shaking free one's dormant energies, and through spontaneous dance and silent sitting, allowing these energies to be redirected inward.

OSHO Nadabrahma Meditation: A method of harmonizing one's energy flow, based on an ancient Tibetan humming technique.

OSHO Nataraj Meditation: A method involving the inner alchemy of dancing so totally that the dancer disappears and only the dance remains.

OSHO Vipassana Meditation: A technique originating with Gautam Buddha and now updated for the 21st Century, for dissolving mental chatter through the awareness of breath.

OSHO No Dimensions Meditation: A powerful method for centering one's energy, based on a Sufi technique.

OSHO Gourishankar Meditation: A one-hour nighttime meditation, which includes a breathing technique, gazing softly at a light, and gentle body movements.

MORE OSHO BOOKS

Over 7000 hours of talks by Osho have been transcribed into books. If you go to www.osho.com you can sort the titles by subject so you can choose the books that interest you most.

HAMMER ON THE ROCK
Evening Talks with a Modern Buddha

This is a diary of intimate meetings between people of all ages and from all walks of life with a modern buddha, Osho. Here are his responses to their questions on everything from work and relationships to sex, death, and meditation.
This book is full of playful tools to heighten our awareness so that we can both deal with the challenges of everyday life and experience what lies beyond our questioning minds.

ISBN 81-7261-177-3
ISBN 978-81-7261-177-4

ABSOLUTE TAO
Talks on Fragments from Tao Te Ching by Lao Tzu

Osho says speaking on Lao Tzu is like speaking on himself, and you can feel this throughout the book. Tao, like Osho, is the way of wholeness – not dividing anything, not denying anything, simply remaining choiceless and aware.
Rather than reading this book, you will find yourself listening to it as if it were a waterfall. And as you listen, you will come to understand why Osho and Lao Tzu emphasize hollowness, emptiness. When you can be nourished by emptiness, you are in touch with the eternal. And this connection with the eternal comes through a dancing being. The more you dance outwardly, the more an inner dance becomes possible and the inner emptiness becomes blissful, ecstatic, eternal.
First published as *Tao: The Three Treasures*, Vol.1.

ISBN 81-7261-148-X
ISBN 978-81-7261-148-4

And Now and Here
Beyond the Duality of Life and Death

Most of us look for security in our relationships, in our choice of living and working conditions, and in our finances. Underlying this search for security is a deep, instinctive fear of death, which continually colors our lives and drives our focus outward, toward survival. But we also have a longing to turn inward, to relax deeply within ourselves, and experience the sense of freedom and expansion this brings.

With this book we can start exploring our inner world without fear. Osho debunks our myths and misunderstandings around death and invites us to experience our eternal inner space – now and here – through guided meditations at the end of the first chapters. One of these meditations has been recorded with music and included as a CD with this book. Called Relaxing the BodyMind Meditation it is a gentle yet profound process and technique that can be used again and again to deepen our experience of awareness and relaxation.

This book is available for the first time in hardcover format, combining the original two volume paperback version into one beautiful volume.

ISBN 81-7261-212-5
ISBN 978-81-7261-212-2

The Book of Secrets
112 Keys to the Mystery Within

In *The Book of Secrets* we are invited to experience and experiment with the games and situations that everyday life brings through the tools of our senses. The 4000-year-old Vigyan Bhairav Tantra is a compendium of highly condensed, telegraphic instructions for 112 different awareness techniques that bring us into the present moment. Osho describes each technique in detail, and explains how we can discover which is the best one for us and how to integrate it into our daily lives.

"These techniques, if followed, suddenly turn your mind. It comes to the present. When the mind comes to the present it stops, it is no more. You cannot be a mind in the present, that is impossible." Osho

ISBN 81-7261-217-6
ISBN 978-81-7261-217-7

THE ART OF DYING
Talks on Hasidism

Osho speaks on classic Hasidic stories compiled by the Jewish philosopher, Martin Buber – a great tradition of laughing saints and wonderful stories.

"Death and life are two polarities of the same energy, of the same phenomenon – the tide and the ebb, the day and the night, the summer and the winter. They are not separate and not opposites, not contraries; they are complementary. Death is not the end of life; in fact, it is a completion of one life, the crescendo of one life, the climax, the finale. And once you know your life and its process, then you understand what death is." Osho

ISBN 81-7261-108-0
ISBN 978-81-7261-108-8

LIVE ZEN
A New Therapy Is Born – Therapy through Gibberish

In this small, potent book, Osho leads us through the mysterious world of the ancient Zen masters. When illuminated by his words and silences, what at first look like insoluble riddles become doorways to the beyond.

During this series of talks the OSHO No-Mind Meditative Therapy is also born. To know the no-mind of Zen, says Osho, we must first rid ourselves of all the garbage and repressions that our overloaded minds have carried for lifetimes. The cure? A week of one hour of gibberish followed by one hour of silent sitting.

"How long can you go on? The mind becomes empty. Slowly, slowly a deep nothingness…and in that nothingness a flame of awareness. It is always present, surrounded by your gibberish. The gibberish has to be taken out. That is your poison." Osho

ISBN 81-7261-207-9
ISBN 978-81-7261-207-8

THE MESSAGE BEYOND WORDS
A Dialogue with the Lord of Death

The Kathopanishad is an ancient Indian scripture that addresses the reality of death and the dimensions beyond it. It tells a very sweet teaching story about an innocent boy, Nachiketa, and his search for the secrets of the soul as he confronts and questions Yama, the Lord of Death.

Here Osho turns the eye of enlightenment on the fear and misunderstanding that surrounds death in the modern mind.

Completely exposing the myth of death, he shares a vision that is both decidedly practical and highly esoteric.

"The Upanishads are unique scriptures on this earth about the mysteries of life, and the Kathopanishad is unique amongst all the Upanishads." Osho

ISBN 81-7261-098-X
ISBN 978-81-7261-098-2

My Way: The Way of the White Clouds

The questions Osho answers in this book were chosen over a period of fifteen days with a specific purpose: to introduce Osho and his work to the thousands of visitors and seekers looking for a new way of life.

With the clarity available only to a man who has gone beyond time and space to a state of supreme consciousness, Osho gives a comprehensive blueprint of his vision for a troubled twenty-first century humanity.

The symbol of the white clouds is chosen to represent the way a seeker moves on the path, and this book addresses all the states – storms, winds, rains, sun, rain and rainbows – that are part of the adventure.

ISBN 81-7261-218-4
ISBN 978-81-7261-218-4